NEW MUSEUM ARCHITECTURE

I would like to acknowledge the contributions of time, material, and artwork from the many museum institution press offices, architecture practices, and photographers that participated in making this book happen. Much gratitude goes out to editor Ron Broadhurst and designer Dung Ngo for their invaluable guidance and expertise. I am indebted to the support and encouragement of my friends and family. This book is dedicated to my grandmother, Reva Lazarus.
—M.Z.

First published in the United Kingdom in 2005 by
Thames & Hudson Ltd, 181A High Holborn,
London WC1V 7QX

www.thamesandhudson.com

Design by Dung Ngo
NGOstudio / www.NGOstudio.com

British Library Cataloguing-in-Publication Data
A catalogue record for this book is available from the British Library

ISBN-13: 978-0-500-28580-0

ISBN-10: 0-500-28580-2

Printed and bound in China

Mimi Zeiger

NEW MUSEUM
ARCHITECTURE

INNOVATIVE BUILDINGS
FROM AROUND THE WORLD

With 190 colour Illustrations

Thames & Hudson

The "New": Invention and Reinvention of the Museum

New, more than other related adjectives such as *recent* or *contemporary*, does not so much fix a subject in time—thus linking it to a historical sequence—as it purports to wipe that very history clean. Using a "Brand New" Swiffer and a squirt of "New and Improved" Windex, the fogged lens of history is polished and buffed to a point where its gleam obscures all that came before. Modern architecture thrives on this reactive optimism. In his Futurist Manifesto, written in 1909, poet and theorist Filippo Tommaso Marinetti derided museums as cemeteries, calling them "Truly identical in their sinister juxtaposition of bodies that do not know each other." Advocating the razing of moribund cultural institutions, he wrote, "Let the good incendiaries with charred fingers come! Here they are! Heap up the fire to the shelves of the libraries! Divert the canals to flood the cellars of the museums! Let the glorious canvases swim ashore! Take the picks and hammers! Undermine the foundation of venerable towns!" In Marinetti's view, the future of architecture, the new, is antithetical to preservation and collecting, to the morbid tombs that make up cities, requiring a clean slate.

The early part of the twentieth century is littered with spent tabulae rasae, with each successive avant-garde movement proclaiming the past dead. Le Corbusier's epitomic Contemporary City for Three Million People (1922) and the later Plan Voisin (sited within Paris's antique center) patterned the sprawling landscape in an efficient and clean geometry of green space, asphalt, and concrete skyscrapers raised on *pilotis* to create a unified ground plane. His 1939 Museum for Unlimited Growth proposed a square spiral, also lifted on the signature *pilotis*, neutrally extending toward infinity. Stressing the rejuvenating and expansive power of the new, Mies van der Rohe's New National Gallery (1968) in Berlin is the built culmination of his collage and drawing studies of reductive museum architecture. Mies's concept of "universal space" is predicated on an open floor plan barely broken by planar partitions displaying the art. Additional galleries and support spaces are hidden below. A temple to modern art, the minimal steel and glass pavilion sits on a wide podium above the city—the raised

Opposite: Guggenheim Museum, Bilbao, Spain. Frank Gehry, 1997. Exterior view

Left: New National Gallery, Berlin, Germany. Mies van der Rohe, 1968. View from plaza   *Right*: Centre Pompidou, Paris, France. Renzo Piano and Richard Rogers, 1977. Place Beaubourg facade

plaza fills the field of vision and paints a purist landscape across postwar Berlin's ragged canvas.

Even the populist Centre Pompidou by Renzo Piano and Richard Rogers (1977) employs a "clean slate" philosophy. A sloping plaza meets the technological exuberance of Piano and Rogers's building; the trust in function is seen in the exposed piping and whimsical escalators climbing up the facade. That square, the Place Beaubourg in Paris's Marais district, gathers the requisite street musicians and jugglers in front of the building, but it is also recontextualized by the machine-like structure. No longer a historical rent in the urban fabric, it is reenvisioned as a singular surface, wiping away musty precedent with a new ideology and future visions.

Like mass-marketed cleaning solution, unnaturally blue and sparkling on supermarket shelves, there is something misleading in avant-garde claims to newness. The sincere optimism creates verisimilitude, but the new, for all its fresh promise, must reconcile itself with the past. In this sense, the new museum is still struggling with old architectural conceits. Despite the desire for tabulae rasae, the context creeps in again and again. Existing buildings, landscapes, and urban histories tether the urge toward purely formal investigations.

Frank Gehry's design for the Guggenheim Museum Bilbao (1997), among other things, epitomizes the struggle and symbolic relationship between form and context. An expressionist gesture in an industrial city, the museum's titanium shapes blossom against Bilbao's period cornices and darkened smokestacks. The shiny metal swoops are natural extensions of innovative building techniques. To create the spectacular surface, computer-aided lasers individually cut each of the singular panels. The result is a starburst of new made newer, and even newest, by a cocktail of technology and contrast. In his article "Build It and They Will Pay: A Primer on Guggenomics," Andrew

Friedman critiques this contextual interplay as an expression of cynicism in a global economy. "For [Guggenheim Bilbao's] cataclysmically stacked, collided, and crumpled forms not only pun on the nearby smokestacks and cranes; they seem, incredibly, to be Gehry's whimsical idea of visually rendering the tumultuous and violent process by which a once-working industrial waterfront is brought to heel—an actual enactment of the grim process that the Guggenheim makes a point of capitalizing on."[1]

The capitalization Friedman refers to, with a touch of loss, is the transformation of Bilbao from living city to architectural destination and tourism generator (a phenomenon otherwise known as the "Bilbao Effect," as other cities acquire signature architecture in order to stimulate their own makeovers). Rather than erasing context, as was standard practice for early modernists, the urban fabric is reappropriated. As a spectacle, the Guggenheim Bilbao succeeds in aligning the new with a reconceived building type, the museum.

The Bilbao Effect and Beyond

The museum of the cultural imagination is classical, conservative, and old. Novelty loses out to a palatial stateliness that stems historically from 1793 when Napoleon made public the royal collection at the Louvre. Grand and monumental, the same architectural symbology that marks buildings as important was carried over to this nascent program. Historian and critic Jayne Merkel, in her essay "The Museum as Artifact," writes, "Not surprisingly, palace architecture—grand, classical, urban, and horizontal—was a principal influence when the first museums were designed. But like most public buildings at the time, they were built in the classical style for other reasons as well, including classicism's association with government and law

(Roman basilicas), with the sacred (Greek temples and Italian Renaissance churches), and with the culture and art of the past."[2]

Standard programmatic features like monumental stairs, courtyards, atriums, and naturally lit galleries—design elements that have carried over to the contemporary museum—all were born in this era of museum building. Citing Karl Friedrich Schinkel's temple-fronted Altes Museum in Berlin (1830) and Robert Smirke's British Museum in London (1823–46), Merkel identifies three elements that control and define museum development: "lighting, security, and procession through space."[3]

The heaviness associated with these venerable institutions stems from the Enlightenment-inspired sense of responsibility to educate the public in the ways of civic culture and civic place. James Traub, in his article "The Stuff of City Life," celebrates the enduring substance of New York City's nineteenth-century museums, such as the American Museum of Natural History or the Brooklyn Museum of Art: "The Gilded Age monuments are in many ways archaic places, with an archaic regard for chronology, compendiousness, categorical crispness. But it is this very persistence, or rootedness, that accounts for the deep feelings so many New Yorkers have towards them."[4]

Cataloging and categorizing requires stuff to place in these collections, yet it is precisely the stuff that contributes to archaic stodginess. Cabinets of curiosities, museums are packed to the rafters with Elgin Marbles, arrowheads, Hudson Valley School paintings, or whatever other archival wonders their collections may hold. Honing in on the museum as repository and the auratic value of the pieces housed within, Traub writes, "These companionable places are about things; they are shrines to the particular and irreproducible object. And just as rootedness is a diminishing category now that practically anything can move practically anywhere, so an orientation towards things

Left : Altes Museum, Berlin, Germany. Karl Friedrich Schinkel, 1830. Entrance facade   *Right* : Kunsthaus Graz, Graz, Austria. Spacelab Cook-Fournier (Peter Cook and Colin Fournier), 2003. Roof and city skyline

feels increasingly obsolete in our age of rampant etherealization."[5]

The billon-dollar J. Paul Getty Center (1997) is chronologically a contemporary museum; Richard Meier's off-white high-modernist temple perched above the 405 Freeway in Los Angeles even gives off a whiff of the "new" impulse toward a clean slate. But the nature of the Getty, traditionally absorbed in collecting and conservation, places it in the category of the old. White limestone glares on the outside, while period rooms cloaked in damask and parquet picture galleries march inside as an enfilade. In contrast, the Guggenheim Bilbao has no permanent collection. The sublimely sculptural halls are filled with imported pieces and traveling exhibitions. "It comes off like the New York Guggenheim's garage, filled with outtakes from its vaults and sporadically supplemented with exhibits on such subjects as motorcycles and Gehry himself," gripes Friedman.[6] It is a complaint that speaks to the global effect of the Guggenheim enterprise masterminded by New York Guggenheim Museum director Thomas Krens. At its height, exhibitions would trip through all the museum's satellites: SoHo, Las Vegas, Venice, Berlin, and Bilbao. While both the SoHo and Las Vegas museum outlets have closed, what remains is the fact that the "stuff" of museums post-Bilbao is transitory.

Museum gallery spaces are designed for endless possibilities, and a seasonal fleet of prepackaged traveling shows (and the premade catalogs and press materials that come with them) speed through European and American cities. Endlessly globetrotting, the exhibitions are shipped in, displayed, and sent on their way—the museum is merely a pit stop on the grand tour. Several projects in this survey, such as the Kunsthaus Graz by Peter Cook and Colin Fournier or the Contemporary Arts Center (CAC) in Cincinnati by Zaha Hadid, are freed from the burden of storing collections. No longer cultural cemeteries piling up gilt-framed paintings like

Left : Contemporary Arts Center, Cincinnati, Ohio. Zaha Hadid, 2004. Fifth-floor gallery   *Right* : Guggenheim Museum, Las Vegas, Nevada. Rem Koolhaas/OMA, 2001. Entrance

sarcophagi, these museums face a different programmatic challenge: flexibility. Cook and Fournier address these matters by creating large, unpartitioned exhibition halls under the biomorphic skin of the "Friendly Alien" architecture. The museum calls attention to itself as a happening event space—light displays undulate across the blue, curving surface—and, as at Bilbao, the architecture creates a dialogue between its form and the urban condition. At the CAC Hadid addressed the anxiety of changeability with a whole "collection" of galleries dubbed the "Jigsaw Puzzle": the short, wide, narrow, and tall galleries present a range of possibilities. In both cases, the museum must communicate its importance to the city at large as a cultural destination as well as its importance to the museum organization as the single-largest (and indeed only) sculptural piece in the museum's collection.

"Museums are sanctimonious Junkspace; no sturdier aura than holiness," writes architect Rem Koolhaas in his essay "Junkspace." Echoing Marinetti's metaphor of morbidity, he continues, "Dedicated to respect mostly the dead, no cemetery would dare reshuffle corpses as casually in the name of current expediency; curators plot hangings and unexpected encounters in a donor-plate labyrinth."[7] Unlike the Futurists, though, Koolhaas rails against museums because of their endless shifting and flexibility, not because of their entombed artifacts. For Koolhaas, Junkspace— completely air-conditioned yet undefined, semi-spectacular, and wholly commercial—is pandemic, a condition that describes malls, airports, office parks, and even museums. Experientially it is overwhelming and banal. As Koolhaas puts it: "Junkspace is best enjoyed in a state of post-revolutionary gawking."[8]

Koolhaas's critique is part observation of what he sees as the contemporary condition and part self-critiquing irony. The architect's contributions to the world of

Left: Museum of Modern Art, New York, New York. Philip Goodwin and Edward Durell Stone, 1939; Philip Johnson, 1950 and 1964. Fifty-third Street facade   *Right*: Museum of Modern Art, Queens (MoMA QNS), Long Island City, New York. Michael Maltzan, 2004. Rooftop signage as seen from subway

new museums—his small-scale Guggenheim Hemitage Museum (which attaches artwork to movable walls with magnets) and the now-closed Guggenheim Las Vegas (shuttered with a billboard-sized supergraphic)—both sit within the kitschy Venetian Casino, the ultimate in Junkspace. His argument sums up nicely the adjusted museum typology. It highlights endless changeability as not only a convenience but as a new model. Additionally, he points out that this new model is not solely an architectural evolution but a change predicated on consumerism. "Throughout Junkspace old aura is transfused with new luster to spawn sudden commercial viability," writes Koolhaas.[9]

The theoretical rhetoric may be new and improved, but the phenomenon Koolhaas points to is not endemic just to our time: it is a trend sprung from the nineteenth-century availability of cheap printing and popular postcard souvenirs. This "fad" for museums to attempt to bridge the gulf between high and low culture with exhibition memorabilia even finds roots in the most august of modern art institutions, the Museum of Modern Art (MoMA) in New York. In scanning MoMA's history—from 1939, when Philip Goodwin and Edward Durell Stone first landed the museum on West Fifty-third Street, to November 2004 and the opening of Yoshio Taniguchi's elegantly tailored expansion—Philip Johnson's 1964 addition stands out as a paradigm shift in the relationship between the museum and commodity.

Save for the steel-framed arches, the expansion was undistinguished; yet, along with new galleries, the program included a café and a museum store. "[It] marked the beginning of an important trend in museum building—the creation of spaces to attract visitors and raise money rather than to display objects," writes Merkel.[10]

As a brand, MoMA represents a refined sensibility as cool as a four-color lithograph by Jackson Pollock rolled up in a poster tube emblazoned with the MoMA logo. The draw of its retail space is so strong that when the museum relocated to Queens during construction of Taniguchi's expansion the MoMA Design Store remained in Manhattan, spawning a second outlet in SoHo. No longer hawking just tote bags and umbrellas, the museum store displays a sophisticated selection of designer objects; authored by Marc Newsom, Philippe Starck, or Karim Rashid, the products often seem on the cusp of being acquisitioned by the institution.

Michael Maltzan's designs for the lobby and rooftop of the temporary Museum of Modern Art, Queens (MoMA QNS), cashes in on Brand MoMA. The most striking feature of the structure—a boxy, converted Swingline stapler factory—is the rooftop billboard. Designed in collaboration with graphic designers Two Twelve, the signage spells out the MoMA QNS logo amidst the air-conditioning units and water towers that crown the factory building. Riding the Number 7 elevated subway, which connects Manhattan to Queens, the logo is disjointed from afar, but the jumble snaps into alignment as the train pulls into the museum's station. The fragments form a witty play on Cubist forms (the kind of works hanging in the galleries). Yet the billboard also signifies MoMA's stately urbanism, even when the institution's main facility is indisposed.

Retail brand, tourism generator, or Junkspace: the terms that describe the new museum sound bleak and jaded, like economic perversions. Rolling off the tongues of industry insiders, they take on democratic overtones. "Today, museums are busier and more exciting and attractive. Museums are making art available to more and more people," says Arthur Rosenblatt, former vice director of the Metropolitan Museum of Art and now principal with RKK&G Museum and Cultural Facilities Consultants, in an interview with *Building Design & Construction Magazine*.[11] Bullet-pointed in the same article are "7 New Trends in Museum Design." Ticking them off, there are the three familiar items plus a few new ones: "1. Museum structure as

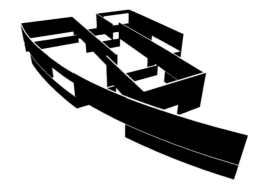

Left: Bellevue Arts Museum, Bellevue, Washington. Steven Holl, 2000. Rooftop sculpture court
Right: Contemporary Art Museum, St. Louis, Missouri. Allied Works Architecture, 2002. Axonometric rendering

artwork and attractor, 2. Greater emphasis on retail space and restaurants, 3. Grand halls for hosting events, 4. Flexible gallery space for traveling exhibits, 5. More outdoor art and landscaping, 6. Hardwiring for technology, 7. Parking becomes a top priority."[12] In sketching out a new conception of the "museum," the points on the list take on a benign clarity, describing positive directions architecturally, socially, and economically in museum construction. Many, if not all, of the projects surveyed in this volume display one or more of these factors. Although shopping, parking, and fundraising seem to dominate, other elements, such as community outreach and civic interplay, are shaping multiple newer typologies.

New "New Museum" Typologies

In a post–Bilbao Effect age both signature architecture and the commercial viability it endeavors to achieve are taken for granted. They reveal a populist role for the museum—one that may even have been built into the substrata of museum history when Napoleon opened up the Louvre (although the display of private collections and dispensation to donors is still widespread). Elitist hauteur is taken down a notch or two via small architectural moves and program additions such as education facilities and studios. For example, Steven Holl's Bellevue Arts Museum is designed around the museum's mission, which focuses on education. The program includes community art classrooms, a ceramics studio, artist-in-residence studio space, and a library. The central atrium collects the various programs. Atriums are a feature so commonplace that Koolhaas derides all museums as "atrium-ridden," but Holl refers to this space as a "social condenser"—a space that attempts to build community rather than give into Junkspace's existential blankness.

With a nod to the inclusiveness now programmatically hardwired into new museum typologies, the projects in this volume loosely group into three categories: "Civic Pavilion," "Regional Response," and "Objet d'Art." Illustrating the "Civic Pavilion," the Contemporary Art Museum in St. Louis, Missouri, conceives of the museum as inextricably linked to its urban context. Designed by Allied Works Architecture, the building physically interacts with the community.

A gently curved concrete wall pushes to the edge of the site, emphasizing the street. Breaking down the barrier between the museum and the city, two large windows provide grand views into the galleries from one and into a classroom from another. Architecturally the openings offer transparency, but conceptually they underline the Contemporary Art Museum's goals of outreach to the city, encouraging education and redevelopment. The building relishes its role as a civic institution without relying on large-scale monumentality.

The formal beauty of the Echigo-Matsunoyama Museum of Natural Science describes one aspect of "Regional Response," the organic relationship between site and structure. Designed by Takaharu + Yui Tezuka Architects with structural engineer Masahiro Ikeda, the museum was commissioned in 1997 for the Echigo-Tsumari Art Triennial, the largest international art event in Japan. The festival uses site-specific artworks and architecture to bring cultural exchange to this rural area. The museum acts as a "stage" during the festival and is open year-round as an innovative natural science center. The rusty steel form that limns the contours of a terraced rice paddy, finishing in an exuberant tower, seems more like a landscape sculpture than a museum. The building takes its hulking shape from the heavy snow loads it carries six months out of the year. A second aspect of the category illustrated in this project is its presence on a larger civic scale so that the museum becomes a landmark for the region.

Left: Echigo-Matsunoyama Museum of Natural Science, Matsunoyama, Japan. Takaharu + Yui Tezuka Architects, 2003. Exterior *Right*: Dia:Beacon, Beacon, New York. Robert Irwin and OpenOffice Art + Architecture Collaborative, 2003. Gallery view with Donald Judd sculpture, *Untitled* (1976). Art © Judd Foundation. Licensed by VAGA, New York, NY

If the category "Objet d'Art" immediately brings to mind the Guggenheim Bilbao, ideally it would be due to the spatial synthesis between Gehry's design and Richard Serra's sculpture *Snake*, where the line between subject and object gently blurs and the two read as a whole. The Dia:Beacon, designed for the Dia Foundation's permanent collection by OpenOffice in collaboration with artist Robert Irwin, similarly blends the artwork with the building. Subtle variations of light or perceptual shifts emphasize artworks by Serra, Donald Judd, and Walter De Maria. A renovated Nabisco printing plant, the museum emphasizes minimalism over sculptural flourish, but flourishes are present (this is no "found" art space) and the architecture is artistic in its own right.

The diversity of subject and form represented by the thirty-one museums—all constructed after 1998—comprising this survey may quell fears of titanium mini-Guggenheim satellites sprouting across the globe. Cursing "cemetery" art museums (both new and old) and calling for their demise no longer seems germane. Not only do the museums display modern and contemporary art, science, natural history, botany, papermaking, stonework, folk art, city heritage, landscape, volcanoes, and archaeological sites, they architecturally engage their context, urban or rural, with a sensitivity that refuses to bore, alienate, or pander to the public. The democratic and pluralistic nature of the new museum comes from this variety. Ultimately, there are as many versions of the new as there are museums.

Contemporary Art Museum
St. Louis, Missouri 2002

Allied Works Architecture (Brad Cloepfil)

The long, slow arc of the exterior wall of St. Louis's Contemporary Art Museum pushes all the way out to the boundary of its street-side site. A band of sidewalk holds the concrete panels in tension, with a cantilevered wall, wrapped in stainless steel mesh, pushing past the edge of the building and turning the corner to demarcate the entry to the museum. It is both an exuberant gesture and a metaphor. The architecture, in reaching out and embracing the street, enacts one of the major ideas behind the founding of the museum in 1980: to foster a dialogue between the city of St. Louis and contemporary art.

The building's program goes beyond the general catalog of galleries and offices to include a philosophical prerogative to engage the community. In his own description of the project, Allied Works principal architect Brad Cloepfil writes, "A building for contemporary art is a home for the unknown, a vessel for a continuously evolving cultural moment. The architecture must strive to create a physical site of spatial situation that will accommodate and inspire."

The Contemporary neighbors the Pulitzer Foundation for the Arts and sits on land donated by Emily Pulitzer. Although the two museums share the sculpture court that houses Richard Serra's torqued steel sculpture *Joe*, the Contemporary is a more modest building (both in cost and in tone) than Tadao Ando's refined edifice for the Pulitzer Foundation. In fact, the loosely defined galleries are more akin to industrial found art spaces than conventional white cubes. In *kunsthall* fashion, the Contemporary does not have a permanent collection—visiting curators and artists (like Kara Walker and graffiti artist Barry McGee) use the space both as display and as something to react against.

Cloepfil achieves this studied edginess by interweaving two orders of walls. At 12 feet high, the lower set runs east to west. The concrete panels—some clad in gypsum board—are equipped to hang art. Their dimensions casually outline the lobby, the performance space, and the main exhibition hall. Running north to south, the second set of walls act like large beams, spanning the lower order. These elements, more than the lower order, continue the metaphor developed at the exterior. Here, the stainless steel mesh wraps the inside walls, bringing urban textures into the art spaces. Offset ceiling surfaces within the walls create clerestories that bring natural light into the galleries.

Two large windows punch though the curving concrete wall delimiting the building. One, near the corner of the exhibition hall, affords an uncanny transparency all the way through the museum galleries from the busy street to the interior courtyard. The second window—seemingly framing the museum's goals of outreach and community activism—lights the classroom of the education department, whose program is entitled "New Art in the Neighborhood."

Top: Entrance facade
Right: Concrete walls wrapped in stainless
steel mesh are cantilevered over entry.

Above: Exterior sculpture courtyard
Opposite: View from lobby to exhibition space

Gallery with works by Owusu Ankomah (above)
and Zineb Sedira (left)

Pulitzer Foundation for the Arts
St. Louis, Missouri 2001

Tadao Ando

Built to house the modern art collection of Emily and Joseph Pulitzer, the Pulitzer Foundation oscillates between serving its civic duty and reserving a private space for artful meditation. The 27,000-square-foot gallery is Tadao Ando's first public building in the United States—the Japanese architect's Modern Art Museum of Fort Worth, Texas, was completed one year later.

Sited just off Grand Street, and part of St. Louis's cultural redevelopment area, the building shares a sculpture garden with Allied Works's Contemporary Art Museum. A nineteenth-century industrial city ravaged by wrecking balls in the twentieth century (as the suburbs flourished and the core suffered), St. Louis is attempting to reinvigorate its civic center. Ando's architecture reinterprets the meaning of public space, offering up quietude, with a hint of alienation, rather than cloying flash or entertainment. The building defines its urban relationship with an austere freestanding concrete wall. The reductive surface hides the Foundation entrance. A corner volume, the terminus of the long gallery inside, makes no obvious attempt to express entry, yet it establishes, like a foundation cornerstone, a sense of place.

Inside, the building is restrained and self-enclosed. Two narrow wings, linked by the entrance court and a stair to the upper gallery, wrap around an equally narrow open-air reflecting pool. One wing houses the museum offices and library, while the other is a double-height gallery space. Intensifying the building's inwardness, a long, low stretch of ribbon windows look out on a near mirror of themselves across the water in the courtyard.

The main gallery is a 170-foot-long expanse lined in white plaster rather than concrete, Ando's usual material of choice. A broad staircase, nearly the width of the gallery, drops down to a lower level. This change in section creates a minimalist amphitheater in front of Ellsworth Kelly's *Blue Black*, a 28-foot-high piece that was commissioned for the space, with the artist and architect collaborating on its installation. A reveal in the roof above the artwork washes the blue and black aluminum rectangles with ethereal light. Richard Serra's torqued steel sculpture *Joe*, commissioned in honor of Joseph Pulitzer Jr., is installed in the sculpture court that the Pulitzer shares with the adjacent Contemporary Art Museum. Organic yet severe, the spiraled artwork resonates with the architecture.

Though not employed in the main gallery, Ando's signature concrete marks time throughout the building as a gray 4-by-8-foot grid dotted with a pattern of form holes. The material, poured into meticulously precise, plastic-lined formwork and carefully vibrated to achieve optimal smoothness, is free of any imperfection. So perfect is the surface that it resembles a taut screen rather than a solid wall. Against the abstract grid, the visitor's meandering pace and organic form are undeniably human. Perhaps unexpectedly, the modernist architectural rigor provides an opportunity for self-reflection.

Page 25: Reflecting pool between the
museum's two wings
Opposite: Museum entrance
Right: Slit window looking out to entry court
Bottom: Street facade

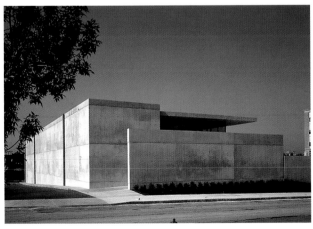

Below: View from gallery toward office wing
Opposite: Ellsworth Kelly's *Blue Black* (2001) in main gallery

Kiasma, Museum of Contemporary Art
Helsinki, Finland 1998

Steven Holl Architects

According to architect Steven Holl, the experience of architecture is the relationship of the body in space to the built environment. At Kiasma, Museum of Contemporary Art, the building is a figurative body negotiating a relationship to a larger urban condition. The museum is sited north of Helsinki's neoclassical center on Mannerheiminte, a wide, ill-defined street lined with autonomous buildings—Alvar Aalto's Finlandia Hall, J. S. Sirén's Parliament Building, and Eliel Saarinen's railway station. The area is a ragged seam where the fabric of the inner city meets an early-twentieth-century suburb. Holl's goal with Kiasma was to use the Museum of Contemporary Art to bind the disparate elements together. It is an ambitious task that stresses design as a means to create a civic sphere.

The word *kiasma* is Finnish for "chiasma," the crossing of two paths or two strings of DNA, and Holl uses it liberally in defining the project. "The crisscrossing of the building concept and an inter- twining of the landscape, light, and the city mark many routes through the museum that involve turns of the body and the parallax of unfolding spaces," writes Holl in his book *Parallax*.[1] The word takes shape formally in the building massing: a brushed aluminum and glass rectilinear block, which reinforces the urban fabric, is crossed with a slow curving volume. The curvy form is made of glass blocks on the concave surface; its bulbous roof meets the ground on the near elevation and is clad in solid zinc mixed with small amounts of titanium and copper.

A statue of Marshal Mannerheim—a key figure in Finland's independence—marks the main entry. The curvature of the facade loosely embraces the equestrian sculpture and creates a parklike setting around a reflecting pool. Inside, the bowed shape rises into a top-lit atrium. Cast in concrete with a horizontal board texture, two white walls come together at a sharp angle; one ramp rises to the second floor and another floats above, forcing the visual inten- sity of an already forced perspective.

While administrative offices and educational functions fill the museum's orthogonal block, twenty-five galleries splay off of the ramps. The warped walls combine with the swell of the roof to create an endless variety of gallery spaces—some lofty with entrances on the diago- nal, others atticlike in a traditional enfilade arrangement. White plaster walls unify the surfaces but produce different tones depending on the type of lighting: translucent and transparent glass and direct and indirect natural light provide the variety of illumination necessary for displaying contemporary art.

Holl's dynamic space is designed to pull the viewer through the space, culminating in the upper-level gallery. The space is transcendent yet reconnects with the urban fabric. Through the northern facade—made of textured brass and glass—there is a view back to Töölö Bay at the center of Helsinki. Holl has written of the museum, "With Kiasma, there is hope to confirm that architecture, art, and culture are not separate disciplines but are all integral parts of the city and the landscape."[2]

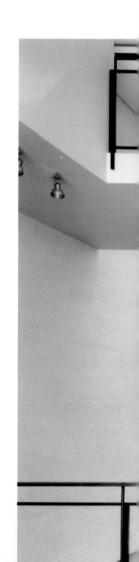

Page 31: Exterior view
Opposite: North facade overlooking Töölö Bay
Below: Double-curved atrium

Below: View down ramp toward entry
Opposite: Third-floor gallery

Contemporary Arts Center (CAC)
The Lois and Richard Rosenthal Center for Contemporary Art
Cincinnati, Ohio 2004

Zaha Hadid

Whether abstracted or literal, a current trend in art museum design is that the architectural form somehow represent if not the collection, then the spirit of the museum collection. Beaux-arts edifices embodying in the most conventional sense an idea of civic responsibility go mute in comparison to architectural signatures that mirror a museum's brand strategy. In her Contemporary Arts Center in Cincinnati, Zaha Hadid was charged with the task of designing a museum with no permanent collection, a situation in which, by default, the building is not only the largest piece of art in the CAC archive, but the only one.

Situated on a corner in downtown Cincinnati, the Rosenthal Center collects the city into the building, forming a cultural nucleus within the community. At every point of its design, the CAC evades being a static object. While bearing some passing resemblance to Breuer's Whitney Museum of American Art, it is not stodgy. The facade displays the diversity of its context, with both the forms and the materials picking up the language of the neighborhood. Raw, precast concrete panels mimic the textures of nearby office towers and the dense mix of smaller, older structures.

The design is generated from the street. In fact, the sidewalk flows into the lobby, sweeping up in a steep curve to form the rear wall. Storefront-like windows lining the ground floor are a minimal impediment to the dialogue between the city traffic and museum visitors. Hadid refers to the dynamic concrete floor as an "urban carpet." A flight of stairs, composed of jittery angles, drops down through the atrium and meets the rush in from the street. The risers are smaller and the treads are wider than a standard stair. Consequently, traversing the stair is closer to the experience of winding up a ramp, a spastic reinterpretation of Frank Lloyd Wright's Guggenheim. Fragmented views of the city beyond are drawn in through atrium windows.

Steel, ramplike stairs float in the atrium. The circulation core, a jagged stack of black bars washed in white light, is a three-dimensional model of El Lissitzky's *Proun* compositions (a famous influence on Hadid's work). The Russian avant-gardist's experimental compositions sought to create a rational space that blended art, architecture, and daily life—a theme carried out in Hadid's structure.

The gallery volumes rise seven stories with the stair to create what Hadid calls a "jigsaw puzzle." The spaces are unpredictable: some are short or wide, others narrow or tall. The architect redefines flexibility by offering up a tremendous variety of exhibition halls, which speaks to the infinite possibilities of contemporary art, representing their boundlessness in a way not possible in white-cube galleries.

Page 37: View of museum from Walnut Street
Left: "Urban carpet" sweeping in from street to lobby
Above: View of ramplike stairs connecting galleries

Below: Atrium

Opposite: Fifth-floor gallery with Iñigo Manglano-Ovalle's titanium sculpture *Cloud no. 1* (2003)

Jewish Museum
Berlin, Germany 1999

Daniel Libeskind

Sited on the Lindenstrasse, adjacent to the baroque edifice of the Berlin Museum, the Jewish Museum Berlin is an artwork, a representation of city history, and a somber memorial. Daniel Libeskind won the competition for the museum design in 1989, and the building was ten years in the making, so technically the design is not new, but is instead a sort of palimpsest mapping a collection of museums designed by the architect in the past decade, including the Felix Nussbaum Museum (1999), in Osnabrück, Germany, and the Imperial War Museum (2002), in Manchester, England.

Questions of recording and remembering Jewish history are encoded in the structure. The zigzag footprint is symbolically derived from a fragmented Star of David. Layered over the plan are lines that trace the address coordinates of sixty key cultural figures who lived in the Lindenstrasse neighborhood before the Holocaust. "In the structure of the building I sought to embody the matrix of connections which might seem irrational today but are, nevertheless, visible and rationalized by relationships between people," explains Libeskind in the book Jewish Museum Berlin. "I attempted to represent the names and numbers associated with the Jewish Berliners, with the 200,000 Jews who are no longer here to constitute that fabric of Berlin which was so successful in business and the arts, intellectual, professional, and cultural fields."[3]

The extension lines of these connections are recorded on the museum facade, in the form of irregularly shaped windows in the surface. Some are delicate crossings, others are gashes or punctures that transform the fenestration into an evocative zinc skin. Inside the museum these openings allow for fragmented views of the city and sky, but in their disjointedness they underscore the unsettled tone of the gallery spaces.

The journey through Libeskind's design begins inside the palatial Berlin Museum. The visitor must descend to the basement level and enter the new museum through an underground corridor. The path's walls and floor slope and converge; at its end are three routes: to the E. T. A. Hoffmann Garden, to the memorial Holocaust Void, and to a stair leading to the galleries. The monumental stair, tightly bounded between its walls, rises all the way through the building, narrowing at its apex and crossed by angled concrete beams.

The Holocaust Void, detached from the body of the museum, is reached through a ground-floor corridor. A hollow concrete tower rises 90 feet (the height of the museum), with the trapezoidal space inside commemorating the devastating horrors of the event. A heavy metal door entraps the visitor in an empty column lit only by a slit high in the tower. The quality of light was designed to recall the slatted light in the cattle cars that shipped Jews to concentration camps.

Libeskind's name for the project is "Between the Lines," and the title manifests in a perfectly straight stroke that penetrates the fragmented composition. Where this line slices the plan, the architect has left seven voids—metaphors for the absence and erasure of Jewish history in Berlin. Delicately illuminated by skylights, the concrete voids are inaccessible, with only small windows giving any trace of their profound presence through absence.

Page 43: Courtyard
Above: Exterior view
Left: Entry to museum through the baroque Berlin Museum
Opposite: Monumental stair leading from subterranean corridor

Left: Exhibition space
Above: View of first of seven "voids"

American Folk Art Museum
New York, New York 2001

Tod Williams Billie Tsien and Associates

West Fifty-third Street in midtown Manhattan is best known as the address of the archetypal cultural institution the Museum of Modern Art (MoMA). Yet that familiar block is also home to the American Folk Art Museum. Surrounded on three sides by Yoshio Taniguchi's redesigned MoMA, the tiny museum stands out like a found artifact, shiny with a little tarnish, in a normative gray grid. Viewed from a plaza opposite, it maintains its *objet d'art* autonomy without resorting to architectural flourishes.

The sculptural, 40-foot-wide facade is composed of folding planes; heavy panels made of Tombasil, a bronze alloy, clad the building. Williams and Tsien's sensitivity to materials and texture is evidenced in the panels. The liquid metal was cast on the concrete floor of the foundry, so that fossil-like pits and cracks were formed in the surface. The material, darkly gleaming on the front of the building, reveals its own making and craft like much of the folk art contained inside.

Resembling a town house in scale, the museum interior is a study in density and utility. The architects managed to fit in the requisite museum café, bookstore, offices, and auditorium along with four levels of galleries. The west side of building serves as the stair and elevator core. In spite of the compact site, there is remarkable expansiveness. Upon entering the museum, the volume opens up in an 85-foot-high atrium. Natural light pours down from a skylight, illuminating a varied materials palette of concrete, recycled wood, and fiberglass. The building's intimacy, combined with its complex, vertical spatiality, recalls the early-nineteenth-century house-museum of Sir John Soane in London. In both projects an interwoven section relieves the condensed architectural massing.

Williams and Tsien conceived the museum experience as a journey, and their concept is reflected in multiple circulation paths in the upper galleries. A secret, wooden stair runs between the fourth and fifth floors. Yet it is the grand staircase bridging the third and fourth floors that is the most surprising. The flight is seemingly out of place—so broad that it would most conventionally be on the first floor—but it opens up an opulent volume. Galleries wrapping the stair peer onto the resulting light well. Openings in the dividing wall frame a collection of weathervanes that hang in the space. A visitor traveling through the museum gets multiple views of the same object from different vantage points.

Cherry-wood handrails on the stairs represent only one detail among many that illustrate Williams and Tsien's evocative use of tactile materials. Shaped by Japanese woodworkers for the project, the tapered and then rounded ends of the rails convey the reassurance of early Americana like baseball bats or rolling pins. Their craft, like the making of the museum itself, is redolent of folk art but devoid of nostalgia.

Cushman/Danziger Family Atrium

Page 49: Fifty-third Street facade
Left: Staircase from ground-floor gallery
Above: Detail of stair

Opposite: Fourth-floor atrium
Above: Second-floor gallery with view of mezzanine

Museum of Modern Art, Queens (MoMA QNS)
Long Island City, Queens, New York 2002

Michael Maltzan and Cooper, Robertson & Partners

The master plan of the Museum of Modern Art, Queens, derived from the simple need to set up a temporary location while Yoshio Taniguchi's redesigned MoMA was constructed. The project brief called for moving the venerated Manhattan institution to Long Island City, and the conceptual design challenge posed by the new provisional location was how to maintain a link to the West Fifty-third Street address while letting the museum loosen up a bit. "Brand MoMA"—the collection, the café, the design store, and the logo—long ago established the rules for how an art museum should conduct itself. Although it acquired P.S. 1 (a former public school refurbished into a hip, contemporary art space), MoMA is a luxury brand of art patronage, disconnected at this point from anything but the most refined urbanism.

Michael Maltzan's design incorporates the recognizable identity of Brand MoMA but gives it a new context and a new audience. From the elevated subway line that links Manhattan to MoMA QNS, a shallow relief of water towers and billboards contours the skyline as the museum comes into view, revealing a fragmented supergraphic of the MoMA logo (designed in collaboration with graphic designers Two Twelve). When the train arrives at the station, the letters line up, neatly establishing the institution's presence in Long Island City.

Outside the Thirty-third Street station and onto the street, the urban context is a lively mix of small businesses, greasy spoons, and light industrial buildings. In an interview in *Architectural Record*, Maltzan described the area as "a place of commerce and exchange, constantly in flux . . . a middle landscape, somewhere between urban and suburban."[4] An overhead path of cantilevered fluorescent lights leads the visitor through the flux of the street to the main entrance. A converted Swingline staple factory, the museum building is boxy and windowless. The bright blue facade is broken by a former loading dock, which serves as the entry; the glass doors are sandblasted with the MoMA QNS logo.

Inside, visitors ascend a tight stair and then turn more than ninety degrees to descend a slow, catwalk-like ramp. The requisite café and store occupy decklike structures flanking the ramp at the same skewed angle. Projecting into this transition area between the services and the banal galleries is a white volume that floats above the ticket desk: the "Project Space" is the butt end of a fluid, ramped exhibition space, a white box winking at the white box nature of the museum.

Maltzan's firm designed the public spaces, including the lobby and roofscape, while the firm Cooper Robertson was responsible for transitioning the old building into a secure, leak-proof structure. Since the collection moved to its permanent home, the building has been maintained as a storage facility for the museum.

Page 55:
Top: The jumbled MoMA logo on roof
Bottom: Rooftop signage seen aligned from subway

Above: Museum entrance
Right: View toward information desk, cloakroom, and café

Above: Museum lobby with floating "Project Space"
Opposite: Gallery entrance with ramp to "Project Space"

Museum of Modern Art (MoMA)
New York, New York 2004

Yoshio Taniguchi (Kohn Pedersen Fox, executive architects)

Urbane and sophisticated, the Museum of Modern Art is the quintessential Manhattan institution. Yet a series of additions onto Philip L. Goodwin and Edward Durell Stone's 1939 classically modernist design—in 1951 and 1964 by Philip Johnson and by Cesar Pelli in 1984—left the building in a jumble and still undersized for the museum's collection. The original domestically scaled gallery spaces clashed with Pelli's escalator-filled glass atrium. Japanese architect Yoshio Taniguchi tackled the complex task of MoMA's expansion and renovation with a modernist's straightforward attention to details, materials, and spatial relationships.

Neither an extreme makeover nor a piece of flashy, signature architecture, the MoMA is interwoven into its midtown context with remarkable subtlety. "I approached the project as if it were an urban design. As opposed to designing one thing of beauty, I designed a museum within a city—a city within a city," Taniguchi explained in an interview with Terence Riley, chief curator for MoMA's Department of Architecture and Design.[5] A new entry on Fifty-fourth Street and a lobby connecting to Fifty-third Street are essential to the architect's urban vision for the museum. The once single-sided museum now has two facades. One is a lineup of the building's history: the renovated Goodwin/Stone and Johnson elevations organized by Taniguchi's black granite, aluminum, and glass addition. The other is a looser composition that integrates the competing scales of Johnson's iconic 1953 sculpture garden and Pelli's soaring apartment tower and also creates an entry portico to connect the museum to the street.

A single line of white columns guides visitors through a public space with ticket booths and information desks. The atrium, intricately woven with bridges and balconies, creates elegant interplay between the art, the garden, and the urban environment. "The building reinforces the experience of looking at art. For all of the views of the city, for all the soaring spaces, for all of the bridges that cut dramatically across—at the end of the day, he enables you to enjoy looking at art," said MoMA's director, Glenn D. Lowry, of Taniguchi's design.[6]

The atrium also offers cross-sectional views of the gallery levels: Ceilings 22 feet high distinguish the contemporary art galleries on the second floor, reached by a staircase leading up from the lobby. The third floor displays a variety of museum departments: architecture and design, drawing and photography. Arranged chronologically, MoMA's landmark painting and sculpture galleries begin with the Post-Impressionists on the fifth floor and conclude with art from the 1970s on the fourth floor. The sixth floor (topped by skylights) is a flexible space for temporary exhibitions. The spaces recall the intimate scale of the previous building and architecturally canonize the collection.

Page 61: Atrium

Above: Entrance at Fifty-fourth Street
Right: View of atrium looking east toward Fifth Avenue with Barnett
Newman's *Broken Obelisk* (1963–69) and Willem de Kooning's
Pirate (Untitled II) (1981)

Above: Third-floor galleries
Opposite: Painting and sculpture galleries on the fifth floor

Kunsthaus Graz
Graz, Austria 2003

Spacelab Cook-Fournier (Peter Cook and Colin Fournier)

Kunsthaus Graz's biomorphic form comes straight out of the comic-book futures designed by the British architecture group Archigram. While it physically resembles *Walking City* (1964), designed by group member Ron Herron, its utopian spirit is a direct extension of *Instant City* (1968), designed by members Peter Cook, Dennis Crompton, and Herron. In that project a zeppelin (named *Rupert*) floats to provincial towns bringing with it the instant, happening culture of metropolitan life.

In Graz, *Rupert* has landed, tucked between the old clock tower and the banks of the Mur River. The opening of the Kunsthaus coincided with the small Austrian city serving as the 2003 Cultural Capital of Europe. Cook and Colin Fournier's psychedelic fantasy is as sublimely baroque as the eighteenth-century pastel-colored city. The design integrates the early cast-iron Eisernes Haus (built in 1852) into the museum, and the synergy between the two conditions is palpable and perhaps able to culturally activate the somewhat down-on-its-heels urban area.

The controlled ooze of the structure is clad in a blue Plexiglas membrane that is an experiment in technological optimism: Mounted above the waterproof building casing are 930 circular fluorescent lamps, which are topped by a grid of curved acrylic panels. Each lamp can be separately turned on and off or dimmed, thus acting like a computerized pixel. Developed by the Berlin firm Realities: Unlimited, the system is named BIX, short for big pixel, and has the ability to broadcast simple text, graphics, and animations across the amoeboid screen so that the building's skin acts as a display screen communicating the museum's aesthetic intentions to the city.

Glazed at ground level, the building offers literal transparency between street activities and the museum café and foyer. From this level a travelator takes the visitor up though a soft underbelly and into the gallery, called Space 02. From here, a second retro-techno travelator launches diagonally through the room to arrive in Space 01, the main exhibition hall. A simple stair leads to an additional gallery space, the "Needle." Its elongated form, rounded at the ends, cantilevers off the side of the blob; a window-wall provides a panoramic view over the Old Town.

Space 01 is located under the full curvature of the bulbous roof. Intended for temporary exhibitions and installations, the gallery is left unpartitioned. On the exterior sixteen "nozzles" resembling tentacles emerge from what Cook dubs the "Friendly Alien." Through these sci-fi oculi northern daylight funnels into the exhibition hall. The nozzles are equipped with louvers to modulate the amount of light, and their sidewalls are equipped with rings of fluorescent tubing. Some of the nozzles are directed to catch views as well as light: the flourishes of the clock tower are framed within the avant-garde context, linking the spectacles of two eras.

Page 67
Top: View of "Needle" and "nozzles"
Bottom: Roof and city skyline

Above and opposite, top: The BIX (Big Pixel) system creates animations across the museum facade
Opposite, bottom: Detail of fluorescent "pixel" under Plexiglass skin

Opposite, top: Gallery "Space 02"
Opposite, bottom: Gallery "Space 01" under nozzles
Right: View from "Needle" exhibition space
Below: Gallery "Space 02" with travelator

Museum of Modern Art — Ludwig Foundation (MUMOK)
Vienna, Austria 2001

Ortner and Ortner

A black basalt figure rising out of the Viennese paving, the Museum of Modern Art (MUMOK) is one of three new structures inserted into the museum quarter: MUMOK together with the white limestone box of the Leopold Collection and the elongated, brick Kunsthalle create a studied composition on a historically delicate site. The courtyard of Fischer von Erlach's imperial stables houses this trio of museums. Built in 1716, Erlach's baroque building is located directly across the Ringstrasse from the Hofburg imperial palace (itself flanked by Gottfried Semper's identical natural history and art museums).

From the Ringstrasse the new interventions are barely seen. Ortner and Ortner's original scheme, for which they won the 1986 competition, proposed a nearly 200-foot-tall library tower—an emblem of a contemporary life within the picturesque city. However, the controversial tower plan was canceled, and the three buildings are now buried in the urban fabric so that the courtyard functions as a secret exterior room. Entry into the museum quarter is through the main gate of the Fischer von Erlach stables.

Aligned with the grid of the residential district behind it, MUMOK juts at an angle into the courtyard like the prow of a boat. The museum is entirely clad in basalt lava hung from an internal concrete and steel frame; the facade and the surface of the double-curved roof are the same material. Small details, like larger panels at the top of the building than at the bottom and curved corners that sharpen to right angles at the roof, distort the natural perspective and scale—the building's stature hypertrophies.

Mimicking the grid of the Semper museums, the Leopold Collection also angles into the courtyard, but to a shallower degree. That building and MUMOK frame the neobaroque riding school, renovated to be part of the Kunsthalle. A broad stone staircase rises between the riding school and the modern art museum, leading to the main entrance halfway up the side of the black monolith. Although the lobby is also clad in basalt, inside the dark stone gives way to brightness in an atrium crossed by cast-iron bridges on three levels. Two additional floors are beneath the entry level.

The entrance hall and elevator bank divide the museum footprint into two types of galleries: large, columnless, flexible rooms on one side, and smaller, more traditional rooms on the other. This division takes into account the need to display sculptural and media installations while still maintaining picture galleries. The uppermost gallery is lit by a skylight in the slow curve of the ceiling. Here a single panoramic window reconnects the introspective museum back to its historical surroundings.

Page 73: Basalt-walled atrium
Above: Exterior view from museum quarter
Opposite: Atrium

Above: Top-floor exhibition hall
Opposite: Gallery at entry level

Kunsthaus Bregenz
Bregenz, Austria 1997

Peter Zumthor

A minimal, pearl-gray box sitting on the edge of Lake Constance, the Kunsthaus Bregenz maintains a striking but blurry physical profile. Behind the gridded facade of etched glass panels are hints of a building taking form—horizontal bands of walls or floor slabs and receding volumes. Architect Peter Zumthor has written that the building "absorbs the changing light of the sky, the haze of the lake, it reflects light and color, and gives an intimation of its inner life according to the angle of vision, the daylight, and the weather."[7] The museum emerges as a hazy object among the public buildings lining the esplanade.

Zumthor's design breaks the Kunsthaus program into a pair of buildings: one contains galleries for temporary exhibitions (classrooms and storage are hidden in the basement) and the other houses remaining museum functions—offices, library, and coffee shop. While the separation underscores the modernist purity of the art space, the two structures operate as a dialogue across a plaza. The glass cube is urbanized and mediated by the smaller, black-steel structure and the array of café tables at its base. From that café seating outside, diagonal traces of stairways can be glimpsed behind the facade.

The diaphanous skin of the cube gives the illusion of understanding how the building is put together, but in truth it is only a scrim, literally just a daylight filter and weather guard. "It looks like slightly ruffled feathers or like a scaly structure made up of largish glass panels," writes Zumthor. The facade is completely self-bearing. Steel clamps on the space frame hold the glass panels aloft. Each panel slightly overlaps the panel adjacent to one side and the one below.

A modest set of doors opens from the plaza into the ground-floor exhibition space. Arrayed in a Miesian spiral around the edges of the boxy floor plan, three unequally sized concrete walls provide the only structural bearing for the three gallery levels above. Each wall masks a different circulation system: a monumental stair, a freight elevator, and emergency exit stair.

The Kunsthaus may be an object on the outside, but its interior emphasizes subtle atmospherics. In the upper galleries velvety concrete walls limn the perimeter, hiding the curtain wall. Although there are no windows, filtered daylight ethereally fills the exhibition hall. Described by Zumthor as "light trapped in glass," the ceiling is a grid of glass panels suspended on thin rods. A plenum above the ceiling serves as a "light trap." Daylight enters through the curtain wall and is filtered down through the ceiling. Fluorescent lamps, also in the plenum, provide illumination at the center of the floor where the daylight does not reach.

The two light sources create even luminosity but an uneven effect. The edges of the room are subject to the changes in sky: horizontal winter sunbeams, shifting clouds, and bright days. The light in the galleries has a materiality all its own, which enhances viewing the art. Zumthor's technical specificity creates phenomenological experience.

Page 79: Glass Kunsthaus facade and black steel café/library building
Opposite: Staircase rising behind glass skin
Right: Museum seen from across Lake Constance
Below: Detail of glass facade

Above: Stair to top galleries
Opposite: Entrance-level gallery

Tate Modern
London, England 2000

Herzog & de Meuron

Occupying a converted power station, the Tate Modern is sited directly on axis with St. Paul's Cathedral on the south bank of the Thames. Named Bankside, the district (notably the site of Shakespeare's reconstructed sixteenth-century Globe Theater) languished as an industrial wasteland after World War II bombing; its slow move toward redevelopment began in the early 1980s. Many expect the museum to spur revitalization of the area, and much has been said about its role as a tourist attraction—that the art-going event is overshadowed by the shops and cafés that market the Tate Modern product. The Tate Modern brand is a subsidiary of the Tate Gallery, whose collection was, with the opening of the building, divided into two: one modern and contemporary, the other the Tate Britain, which is located in the Tate Gallery's original premises and is the national gallery of British art from 1500 to the present day.

Herzog & de Meuron's minimalist design attempts to sidestep any architectural gimmickry, and as a result it is extremely true to the original building. Any alterations are abstract and understated. Built in phases between 1947 and 1963, the Bankside Power Station was designed by Sir Giles Gilbert Scott—who also created the iconic British red telephone box. The massive, slightly Art Deco brick facade symmetrically flanks a 325-foot-high chimney. The Swiss firm's hand is seen in the "lightbeam," a two-story steel and glass construction that tops the roof and contains the restaurant and auxiliary functions.

The vast Turbine Hall is entered by a long ramp that slides under the main floor to a lower level. The space is enormous. In his essay "Étienne-Louis Boullée Visits the Tate Modern," Adolf Max Vogt notes that like one of Boullée's grand visions, the 1784 design for the Bibliothèque Royale de Paris, the hall is sublime by virtue of its sheer scale.[8] With the giant, grinding turbine machinery absent, the room evokes both optimistic and ominous visions of modernity, a volume that dwarfs individuals in the service of modern art. Herzog & de Meuron intervene with a skylight that runs the full length of the hall. Glowing white light boxes band the side wall and offer views down from the galleries.

The Turbine Hall is left relatively free of artwork, a counterpoint to the three levels of boxy white galleries reached by a cache of escalators in the middle of the building. Three large-scale sculptures by Louise Bourgeois punctuated the space at the museum's opening. From October 2003 through March 2004, Olafur Eliasson's *Weather Project* engaged the hall at an equivalently majestic scale. The work—a representation of sun and sky, in which dazzling artificial light filled the hall and mingled with a fine mist—transformed the space from interior to exterior and underlined Herzog & de Meuron's intention for the hall to be understood as public space.

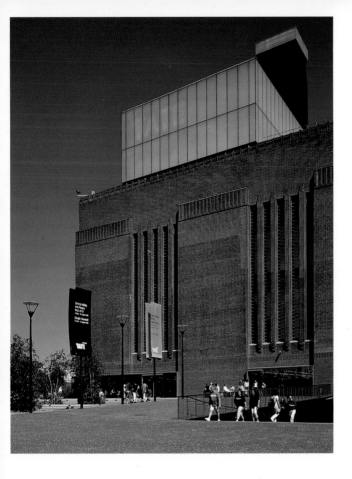

Page 85: Turbine Hall
Above: Glass "lightbeam" atop existing building
Right: Transformed Bankside Power Station from across Thames River

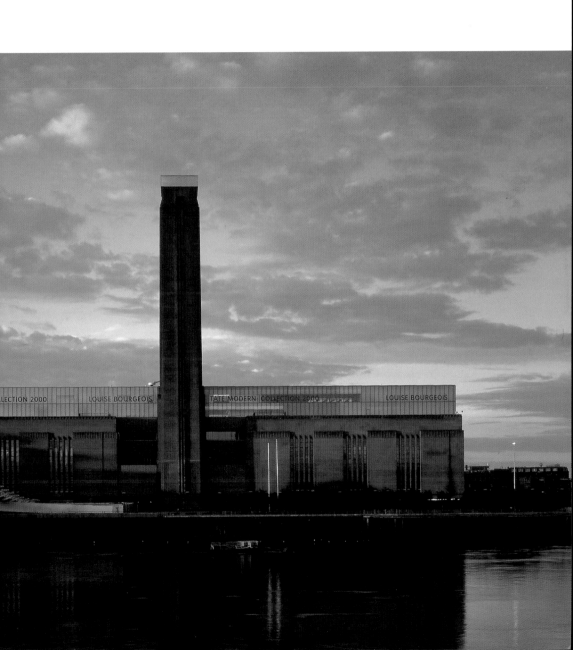

Opposite: Glowing light boxes along Turbine Hall walls
Above: Concourse adjacent to upper-level gallery

Dia:Beacon
Beacon, New York 2003

Robert Irwin and OpenOffice Art + Architecture Collaborative

"The building is now inextricably linked to the art. Our entire purpose in designing the building was to disappear, and make the art seem like it was made for the building and vice versa," says former OpenOffice partner Linda Taalman of the Dia:Beacon.[9] Located an hour north of New York City on the edge of the Hudson River, the museum was designed to house the Dia Foundation's permanent collection.

Artist Robert Irwin collaborated with the firm OpenOffice on the transformation of an old Nabisco printing plant into a contemporary art space. Yet the design goes further than the creation of galleries; the building approaches becoming an artwork itself—part readymade, part conceptual art. As an installation artist, Irwin uses light and perception as his media, and his role was what Dia Director Michael Govan describes as "landscape designer, architect, aesthetic philosopher." His Dia:Beacon masterplan uses the whole 300,000-square-foot building and surrounding landscape as a canvas on which to manipulate the viewers experience.

The entry sequence to the museum imperceptibly changes from casual to controlled. A long driveway opens to a parking lot enmeshed within an orchard. All around the museum Irwin has chosen fruit trees to flower at different times of year. With a subtle change in paving, the grid of trees gives way to a plaza in front of the building. The museum café and bookshop sit to the left facing the river.

The entrance lobby is a condensed space in opposition to the vistas of the Hudson Valley and the vast gallery spaces beyond. Irwin placed two new windows in the south side of the building directly opposite the entrance. These windows produce the perceptual trick of collapsing the distance between the entry and rear walls.

Built in 1929, the industrial structure features broad open spaces and high ceilings that were roofed in rows of north-facing sawtooth skylights. "The building was designed to have natural light evenly distributed in many of the spaces, to facilitate the printers' judgment of the color of the Nabisco boxes. So it was designed for the best possible viewing conditions already," explains Taalman.

The refined industrial character of the building resonates with the work inside. The artists represented, primarily with work from the 1960s and 1970s, ground their work in an investigation of mass-produced materials and questioning gallery neutrality. Under the even light, the large galleries are each dedicated to an artist—massive spaces are dedicated to the twisted, automotive-metal sculptures of John Chamberland, the fluorescent light fixtures of Dan Flavin, or Donald Judd's plywood boxes. A series of Richard Serra's ellipses are installed in a separate wing that sits, temple-like, at the end of Irwin's formal garden. The strong, west light warms the grandeur. Here the brick walls are left unpainted, their color complementing the oxidized steel sculptures.

Page 91: Gallery with Fred Sandback's *Untitled*
(from *Ten Vertical Constructions*, 1977)
Opposite: Aerial view
Above: Museum entrance with view into gallery

Above: Gallery with Walter De Maria's *The Equal Area* series (1976–77)
Right: Gallery with Donald Judd's *Untitled* (1976). Art © Judd Foundation.
Licensed by VAGA, New York, NY

O-Museum
Iida, Nagano, Japan 1999

SANAA (Kazuyo Sejima & Ryue Nishizawa)

Using a minimal number of design elements, the O-Museum is a building of refined reflection: a slightly wavy glass bar, floating in a garden context. Located in the alpine foothills above Iida, an agricultural village, the museum is sited on the castle grounds of a sixteenth-century feudal lord. A *shoin*-style building, deemed historically significant by the Japanese government, is all that remains of the palace complex. (Originally developed for the samurai, *shoin* are wood structures divided on the interior by sliding *shoji* screens.)

Kazuyo Sejima and Ryue Nishizawa's design is modern in an antique context, but the long and narrow building warps and responds to its immediate environment. The shallow curves mimic the landscape contours, yet their inflections also respond to the existing buildings. Displaying feudal artifacts, arms, maps, documents, and everyday utensils, the museum paints a picture of sixteenth-century life in the castle and village. The *shoin*, the largest artifact, is central to the experience.

Lifted off the ground and sheathed in full-height glass panels, the new building is a lens for viewing history. The museum provides changing perspectives of the site from a garden level view to an elevated, analytical understanding of the existing buildings. "The space beneath had to be completely void," Sejima explained in an interview. "I didn't know how to lift it gracefully, much less how to build it at all. I thought that if we used six columns instead of four, maybe we could realize it. Usually, if you try to achieve a large span with only six columns, the result will feel very awkward. But here it is casual."[10]

The informal flow of space moves from the garden and under the hovering museum. Upon meeting the steep mountain incline behind the building, the entry experience changes and grows more austere. A ramp rises to meet the structure, and there is a visual interplay between the visitor and the *shoin*: the antique building is glimpsed through a gap between the ramp and the museum, disappears, and then reappears.

Program determines the quality of the glass facade along the linear plan: It is opaque where archives and other light-sensitive materials are stored. In the entry lobby and lounge the glass is textured with a pattern that resembles the variable density of brushstrokes or wood grain. There are also moments in the pattern where the glass is transparent, framing a view of the *shoin* to emphasize its vernacular construction. The light and dark contrast of infill to structural columns is syncopated with the rhythm of the delicate steel and glass panels of the O-Museum.

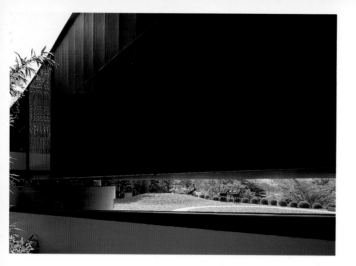

Page 97: Etched glass facade
Above: Exterior view of raised galleries
Right: View of *shoin* from entrance hall
Pages 100–101: Entrance hall

Kalkriese Archaeological Museum Park
Kalkriese, Germany 2002

Gigon & Guyer (with landscape architects Zulauf/Seippel/Schweingruber)

Stretching across farmland in Kalkreise near Osnabrück, Germany, the Kalkriese Archaeological Museum Park makes visible an obscured moment in time. The design traces battle lines dating from 9 A.D., yet evokes the contemporary consequences of war. Not limited to a single didactic building, the "museum" is a series of earthwork interventions and pavilions: the haunted landscape is as much an artifact as any archaeological find.

In the 1980s archaeologists determined the 20-hectare site to be a probable location of the Battle of Varus, a conflict that halted Augustus's imperial expansion into Germany. In 9 A.D. three Roman legions (estimated to be between 10,000 and 20,000 soldiers), led by the general Publius Quinctilius Varus, were ambushed by Teuton fighters under the Cheruscan general Arminius. The Roman regiments, trapped between marshland and forest, were unable to retreat. The Teutons attacked from behind a sod and sand earthwork at the edge of the dense oak and beech wood, advancing and retreating quickly and stealthily through the trees.

Swiss architects Annette Gigon and Mike Guyer poetically mark the battle lines, interweaving them into the agricultural landscape and into the programmatic requirements of the museum. The Roman route of retreat is demarcated by fallen steel plates irregularly placed to symbolize the disarray in the legions' ranks. The snaky extent of the Teuton rampart is tracked along the wooded edge by a row of vertical iron poles. The poles are spaced tighter where archaeological evidence indicates the rampart and farther apart to indicate approximations. Wood-chip paths illustrate the Teutons' swift, camouflaged movements in the forest (which has been replanted to resemble battle conditions).

Outlined by a double wall of sheet-steel pilings, an excavation pit re-creates the historical landscape. At the north of the rectangular cutout the reconstruction of the 16-foot-wide and 5-foot-high rampart is topped with a wattle fence. To the south, on the Roman side, the sandy ground changes to a moor pond.

The museum building Gigon & Guyer placed on this charged site negotiates the landscape with tentative, stilt-like footings. But, sheathed in large Cor-Ten steel panels (roughly 10 by 20 feet), it is still weighty. The structure, designed to orient the visitor to the site, is composed of two elements: a single-story exhibition hall displaying recovered artifacts (with offices and a locker room) and a 120-foot-tall tower. The oxidized industrial panels are interspersed with picture windows at the exhibition hall level. Climbing the tower, the blood-red cladding is left off at irregular intervals, exposing the skeleton and allowing views out over the battlefield.

Three small pavilions dotting the site are significant in constructing a contemporary reading of the historical events, with each dedicated to a different phenomenological experience: listening, seeing, or questioning. The eccentrically morose Listening Pavilion is equipped with an archaic "ear piece." Inside the pavilion the recorded clangs and cries of horses and men in battle are heard. The gramophone-shaped listening device captures real-time sounds of the natural environment. Equally moving and odd is the "eyeball"— a camera obscura framing and distorting the battlefield—protruding from the Seeing Pavilion. The isolated Questioning Pavilion juxtaposes views of the meadow with taped news broadcasts of international conflicts. The final stop on the route through the parkland, the Questioning Pavilion is a poignant reminder that war and loss is not just ancient history but part of the present.

Page 103: Rampart re-created in archaeological pit lined by sheet-steel pilings
Above: Museum building and tower
Opposite: Museum lobby

Above: Seeing Pavilion with "eyeball" camera obscura; steel plates
in ground represent fallen Roman legions
Right: Listening Pavilion with adjustable ear trumpet
Opposite: Interior of Listening Pavilion

Paper Art Museum
Shizuoka, Japan 2002

Shigeru Ban

Architect Shigeru Ban is best known for his paper architecture, so it would seem fitting that he design the Paper Art Museum. Yet his designs, such as the Paper Log Houses, built after the 1995 Kobe earthquake, or the soaring Paper Arch for MoMA's courtyard, are recycled cardboard tube constructs and have little in common with this minimalist museum situated just outside of Tokyo. Two linked structures, the museum and gallery, were commissioned by a Japanese paper manufacturer to house his collection of crafted paper, Japanese graphic design, and contemporary art.

The 4,900-square-foot, three-story museum building is perfectly square in plan and divided into three equal parts, so that two blocks flank a central void. Programmatic functions are divided between the pair of blocks: offices, sample rooms, a lecture room, and a fourth-floor glass penthouse face the south garden; column-free galleries capture the indirect north light. Steel and glass bridges cross the void on the east and west ends, connecting the two blocks. Punctuated only by two rows of structural supports, the ground floor is a single open space.

Wrapped in translucent, fiberglass-reinforced plastic panels, with an interior layer of movable sliding glass panels, the space is completely flexible. The garden surface pivots 90 degrees forming an awning similar to *shitomido*, traditional Japanese vertical shutters. To the west and east, the middle third of each elevation mechanically disappears (on rolling gates), exposing the atrium.

For the contemporary art gallery, Ban renovated the existing single-story, 3,000-square-foot workshop. With the exception of the northwest quadrant, the gallery is a single hall open to the elements. On the south side, six sets of fiberglass-reinforced plastic panels as delicately detailed as *shoji* screens lift on tracks and extend over the terrace to create a sunshade.

These revealing transformations use modern technology to blur the boundaries between interior and exterior space, but they are also historically linked to regional architecture. "The idea was to create a contemporary interpretation of traditional Japanese spaces with contemporary materials," Ban has said of the project. "The size, continuity, and quality of the space can all be changed by means of *fusuma*, *shoji*, or reed blinds depending on the season or occasion. With or without a roof, the interior and exterior spaces are continuous and the intermediate domain shifts depending on the way the space is used."[11]

Parallels have been drawn between Ban's reductive architecture and the concept of "universal space" in the work of Mies van der Rohe. But, finding Mies's work too static, Ban grounds his own work in a theory of open, flexible space, which he calls "universal floor." Capturing the ephemeral qualities of paper, the Paper Art Museum, with its adaptable facades, integrates the outside space into the building, realizing the architect's philosophy.

Page 109: Atrium
Left: Gallery facade with fiberglass panels in open position
Above: Closed gallery facade

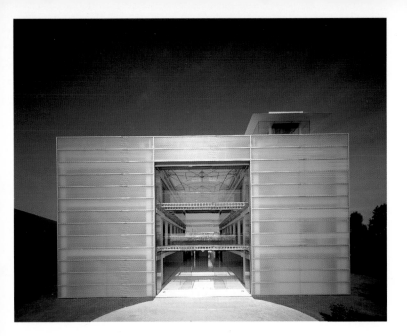

Above: Entrance with three-story retractable facade open
Right: View toward atrium and offices from ground-floor exhibition space

Art Pavilion "De Verbeelding"
Zeewolde, Netherlands 2001

René van Zuuk Architects

The De Verbeelding art pavilion sits on a polder—a piece of manufactured land—jutting out into a small lake. The reclaimed Dutch landscape is a contrivance of nature and technology, a tenuous truce between sea and territorial expansion, and René van Zuuk's design draws from that fragile scenery. The pavilion is the operating base for the De Verbeelding (Dutch for "the imagination"), a center that integrates art, landscape, and nature. It is the one architectural piece in a collection of outdoor sculpture that traces a 4-mile exterior exhibition route through Flevoland, an area encompassing the De Wetering wooded landscape park and across the Randmeren dike. The collection includes works by Richard Serra and Daniel Libeskind.

The narrow spit of land reaching out into the lake was constructed precisely for the pavilion. It is an extension of a main artery through Zeewolde, and it is sited carefully not to compete with the other landscape art but to have its own recognizable presence. The elongated structure, with folding roof planes, appears to float in the water. Its dynamic horizontal form is reflected in the liquid surface, simultaneously doubled and dematerialized.

Serra's piece *Sea Level*, located on the far bank of the lake, aligns with the building and is framed in the narrow glass facade. Van Zuuk cites the long, black concrete walls of Serra's work as one inspiration for the building's stretched form. The structural system is directly derived from traditional Dutch agricultural buildings (called polder sheds). Wooden, three-hinged trusses form each of the three roof-wall enclosures. The trusses are aligned where they meet the ground, but splay open into varying oblique angles as they shape the aluminum-clad roof. While the forms have an organic quality, Van Zuuk stresses the systematic use of conventional technology to produce his "intelligent distortion."

Lightly mimicking the roll of the surrounding terrain, each roof plane independently warps, causing rifts and overlaps. By inserting glass into the resulting fissures, Van Zuuk created clerestory windows to indirectly light the interior. Two freestanding wooden boxes, containing the gallery's support facilities, offices, storage, and toilets, are simply inserted under the shed-like enclosure. The pavilion skin stops short of meeting the ground, leaving a continuous band of floor-level windows. Inside, daylight bounces off the water and illuminates the gallery. From afar, the bent planes hover over the lake, as natural and artificial as the landscape itself.

Page 115
Top: View toward museum entrance
Bottom: View across lake toward northwest facade

Above: Southeast facade
Opposite: Museum offices and entrance

Right: Southwest facade
Below: Glass-enclosed gallery
Opposite: Hinged trusses in gallery

Makino Museum of Plants and People
Shikoku Island, Japan 1999

Hiroshi Naito

Embedded in the contours of Mt. Godia on the island of Shikoku, Japan, the Makino Museum of Plants and People melds with the natural environment. The botanical institute is split into two buildings, one containing a museum and research laboratories, the other containing an exhibition hall. A sinuous path, tracing an approximately 500-foot line east to west across a topographic ridge, connects the structures. Botanical gardens displaying plantings from the Kochi prefecture cover the hilly site.

Named for noted Japanese botanist Dr. Tomitaro Makino, who was born on the island, the museum's library contains a collection of his rare eighteenth- and nineteenth-century botany books. Their pages reveal fine etchings and woodblock prints of Japanese flora. In the organic forms of the inky shoots and unfurling foliage are parallels to Hiroshi Naito's design for the museum. The footprint of the museum/laboratory building is a simple rectangle, topped with a twisting enclosure, but the exhibition hall is curled like a fiddlehead fern.

The leaf-like structures cautiously spread out over the landscape, with both roofs low to the ground and undulating around central, open-air courts. Delicately bent but sturdy, the shelters are designed to withstand the salt winds that buffet Shikoku Island. Steel sections make up the roof ridges and support columns. Laminated Douglas fir trusses and beams—each different to adjust to pitch and roll—follow the roof spine. At the ridge, adjustable ball-and-socket joints provide the flexibility needed to resist typhoon gusts. Zinc and steel panels, engineered and wind-tunnel tested for heavy loads, shield the buildings against wind and rain.

Under the canopy, Kochi-grown cedar (*sugi*) lines the ceiling and lends a warm, red glow to the space. In the exhibition hall a modest number of partitions reach the roof, leaving the spaces interconnected and visually open. Galleries, offices, the library, an auditorium, and laboratories are tucked under roof of the two-level museum building. While the first floor is purely orthogonal, the top-floor rooms organically follow the coiling roof, which extends past the walls and toward the courtyard. Silver-gray Japanese cypress (*hinoki*) is used for a deck that emerges from under the roof structure. A large oval void is left in the terrace to bring light to the green space underneath. From that ground-floor courtyard garden, tree saplings delicately rise and branch out.

Page 121: Terrace
Above and right: Views of terrace and garden

Above and right: Exhibition hall

Echigo-Matsunoyama Museum of Natural Science
Matsunoyama, Japan 2003

Takaharu + Yui Tezuka Architects (Masahiro Ikeda, structural engineer)

Echigo-Matsunoyama Museum of Natural Science sits at the intersection of art, science, and community redevelopment. A hunkering, oxidized form in a terraced rice paddy, it is a landscape piece. Yet, in seeming contrast to the design, the museum also addresses civic concerns. The project was sponsored by the Echigo-Tsumari Art Triennial, the largest international art event in Japan. Begun in 1997, the Triennial stretches over a large rural region on the northwest side of the country, bringing art and culture into the area. Its mission is to use site-specific works to encourage revitalization and artistic exchange between the local population and the participating artists, including international figures such as Jenny Holtzer and James Turrell as well as emerging and local artists. Along with Takaharu and Yui Tezuka's museum pavilion, the Triennial also commissioned the Snow-Land Agrarian Culture Center in Masudai by the Dutch firm MVRDV.

Six months out of the year massive snowfall blankets the Niigata prefecture, which accounts for the fortified profile of the Tezukas' design. The structure twists across the terrain and terminates in a 112-foot-tall tower, which, in the winter, emerges above the snowdrifts. Structurally engineered by Masahiro Ikeda to bear 2,000 tons of snow load, Cor-Ten steel panels, seamlessly welded together and supported by a steel frame, make up the exterior. The placement of the museum on sliders, rather than fixed foundations, allows for structural horizontal expansion.

Extreme weather conditions predicate a wide, ventilated cavity between the exterior and interior walls and required the building to be free of extraneous fenestration. However, at four bends in the floor plan are huge, floor-to-ceiling windows made of 3-inch-thick acrylic, like that used in aquariums. In the winter, drifts form at the windows in icy-white and blue-gray layers of snow against the glass—a seasonal exhibition of natural phenomena.

The museum interior is tubelike, with corridors responding to the bending outside walls. They expand to form the auditorium and café at one end of the building and widen into trapezoidal exhibition halls on the tower side. One gallery is lined with glass vitrines containing butterflies, a celebration of the fantastic spectrum of natural beauty. In another space, two hundred drawers, called "Amusing Boxes," collect the bits of nature—snakeskins, insect shells, and other field specimens—found by visitors in the surrounding meadow and forest.

One hundred and sixty steps lead up a darkened stairwell to the top of the tower. Artists collaborated with the Tezukas to create an installation of sounds and images along the assent. At the apex, the expansive, bird's-eye view over the wooded hills balances the earthy museum experience.

Page 127: Top and bottom: Views of steel-clad facade
Above: View through thick acrylic windows into cafeteria
Right: West facade

Opposite, top: Snow piled up against café window
Opposite, bottom: Lecture hall
Above: Butterfly exhibition room

De Young Museum
San Francisco, California 2005

Herzog & de Meuron

Gussied up in an Egyptian Revival style, the original de Young Museum (then called the Fine Arts Building) was constructed in 1894 for the California Midwinter International Exposition. Since then the original structure weathered earthquakes and additions until it was demolished in 2000. Pavilion-like in its pastoral Golden Gate Park setting, Herzog & de Meuron's building is adjacent to the park's Japanese Tea Garden and looks out across the park's Music Concourse esplanade at Renzo Piano's California Academy of Sciences, due to open in 2008. The new scheme not only offers increased square footage for galleries but strikes a careful balance between its natural and architectural environment.

But what exactly is natural? Although an expansive oasis, Golden Gate Park is surrounded on three sides by city streets and built on top of sand dunes. In the course of its 130-year history plantings completely obscured the original landscape. Herzog & de Meuron's design makes no attempt to restore the original landscape, but the building's skin, in mimicking the effect of light filtered through leaves, continues a tradition of artificial nature. The facade is sheathed almost entirely in copper, which will become muted over time, and each of its 7,200 panels is individually embossed and perforated to create the abstracted pattern. The dimpled, dappled, and filigreed skin filters light into the gallery spaces and also integrates the museum into the site, which is wooded with eucalyptus, Monterey pines, and cypress. A large roof, also made of perforated copper, cantilevers over the sculpture garden. A nine-story tower housing the education facilities links the museum to the greater city context. Dynamically twisting from a rectangle to a parallelogram, it aligns with the park grid at ground level, while at the observation deck it aligns with the city grid.

The de Young's parti—a rectangle slashed into three bands—weaves architecture and green space together. The largest void cut into the plan is the diamond-shaped entry court. The museum facade inflects at the concourse-level, guiding the visitor through a tunnel-like space that offers glimpses of the auditorium seating in the lecture hall and into the courtyard. An as-yet-untitled Andy Goldsworthy piece made of stone from Yorkshire, England, echoes this path by way of a long fissure that runs from the concourse to the entrance doors.

Two slim, tapered gardens, the Fern Court and the Eucalyptus Court, reach into the heart of the building. Nearly meeting, the tense space between the glassed-in points surrounding each court marks the shift from the lobby and main court to the galleries. The grand stair, narrower at the bottom than the top, leads to the large galleries on the second floor and is a place for visitors to gather.

Reflecting the diversity of the de Young collections—ranging from Mark Rothko paintings to Maori sculptures from New Zealand—the architects developed two gallery typologies: nineteenth- and twentieth-century collections are shown in classically proportioned, white volumes with skylights, which glow like the light boxes at the Tate Gallery, indirectly conducting light into the spaces; the Central and South American, African, and Pacific Island galleries are artificially lit and finished in warm wood on the floor and ceiling.

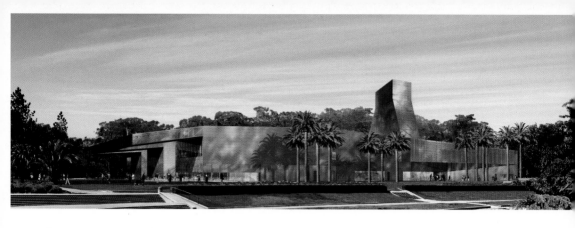

Page 133: Perforated copper panels covering facade
Top: Rendering of museum as seen from Music Concourse
Above: Perforated copper canopy cantilevered over sculpture garden
Opposite: View of San Francisco through tower skin

Vulcania: Parc Europeen du Volcanisme
Saint-Ours les Roches, Auvergne, France 2002

Hans Hollein

Vulcania is an odd combination of natural science, 1960s avant-garde ideology, and theme-park theatrics. A collage of intentions, it is situated in the Auvergne region in France—an area where the landscape was sculpted by hundreds of now-dormant volcanoes. Conceived by former French president Valéry Giscard d'Estaing, the museum's purpose is to celebrate world-wide volcanic research. The mission's subtext is to generate tourism to a region that is economically depressed but rich in pristine natural beauty.

While architect Hans Hollein developed the project prior to Frank Gehry's Guggenheim Bilbao, the "Bilbao Effect"—banking on the entertainment value of museums to transform depressed cities—is clear. There is some coincidence and some irony in the fact that in 1989 Hollein also authored the design for a Guggenheim museum building in Salzburg, Austria, an unbuilt project that proposed carving the museum into the rock of Monchsberg.

Built into the slopes under the extinct volcano Puy du Dôme, Vulcania is a subdued spectacle, with only an iconic, conical structure and the wavy roof of the IMAX theater emerging from a hillside, creating minimal disruption in the verdant, rolling landscape. The rest of the complex is sunken into the earth. "Early human beings sought shelter by digging a depression into earth or by finding a cave," Hollein wrote in a 2003 essay, "Digging and Piling Up,"[12] in which he described the primeval, formal plasticity achieved when carving into the ground.

Descent into the complex follows a walkway along a 600-foot-long wall made of volcanic boulders and past a glass and steel restaurant building. The path flows onto a paved patio that unites the disparate parts of the museum. A cinder cone and a deep crater illustrate the digging and piling up of Hollein's essay. Clad in deep gray volcanic stone, two interlocking half cones rise from the depths of the underground museum. Their interior walls, lined in golden, prismatic, titanium-clad stainless steel, glint and symbolically recall bubbling magma. One hundred feet wide and one hundred feet deep, the crater has been described by the architect as a vision from Dante's *Inferno*. Excavated from the layers of lava flows and bedrock, the walls show the scrapes and gouges of construction. Edging the circumference, a ramp drops underground.

Subterranean exhibition spaces (named evocatively the Rumbling Chamber and Salle Etna) are also dug out of the bedrock, their jagged walls complementing educational dioramas and video installations, including a tableaux of a car trapped in the ash and rubble of Mt. Saint Helens. From this didactic underground space, the visitor emerges into the "Volcanic Garden." Covered by a glass greenhouse, it is filled with lush tropical plants—examples of life returning to an area after an eruption. The space eventually opens above ground, completing the thematic journey and returning the visitor back to the Auvergne landscape.

Page 137: Interior of interlocking half cones
Below: View from crater edge toward museum complex
Opposite: Entrance walkway

Below: View from plaza toward restaurant building
Opposite, top: Subterranean exhibition space
Opposite, bottom: Volcanic garden

Mesquite Heritage Museum and Art Center
Mesquite, Nevada 2003

AssemblageSTUDIO

Located 80 miles north of the spectacles of the Las Vegas strip, Mesquite, Nevada, is a town dedicated to the pursuit of golf. Acres of lush fairways stand out in emerald-green relief against the surrounding desert. Mediterranean-style buildings—clubhouses, spas and twenty-four hour casinos, each with requisite archways and red tile—decorate the resort community. The search for an authentic vernacular vocabulary amid this verdant historicist oasis may seem quixotic, but the Mesquite Heritage Museum and Art Center successfully finds a colloquial language.

Architect Eric Strain of AssemblageSTUDIO drew on the rural agricultural history of the area. Not wanting to overshadow the adjacent Virgin Valley Heritage Museum—a low stone structure dating from 1942—Strain conceived of the project as a "still life" of parts. Central to the composition is a grain silo with an inverted roof, which the architect salvaged from the outskirts of town. Placed in the museum courtyard, it serves as a dramatic performance and gallery space. And while it does not rival the searchlight on top of the Luxor casino in Vegas, when the silo is lit from the inside, light spills out from a reveal in the roof like a beacon.

Several small buildings, each containing a piece of the museum program—galleries, classrooms, lobby, and artist studios—are arranged around the central court. The main gallery is concrete, while the studios and small gallery are clad in weathered steel. A sandblasted glass fence encloses the garden area. "The complex reads from each direction as a collage of dissimilar yet similar structures, which, when combined, read as a single composition," says Strain. "The varying materials come together through the common bond of coming from the earth. The structure, while contemporary in form, appears to have been on site for years."[13]

Although the museum was meticulously designed to fit in with Mesquite vernacular architecture, the materials palette jarred with the design ordinances passed by the Downtown Redevelopment Program. The architect was faced with city codes (requiring hacienda-white stucco) that were intended to preserve a fabricated city history. Across the street from the city hall, Strain's architecture created controversy. The debate, rather than killing the design, ultimately galvanized community support for the museum. "As the building has begun to weather, there is actually more acceptance of the project overall," explains Strain. "You are now able to see the visual connection between the building and the exhibit of farm equipment at the Heritage Museum."

Page 143: View across courtyard toward small gallery
Left: View across courtyard toward silo
Below: Interior of silo
Opposite: Museum entrance

Above: Exterior of large gallery with flexible studios and courtyard beyond
Below: Interior of large gallery
Opposite: Pivot door in small gallery

Luyeyuan Stone Sculpture Museum
Sichuan Province, China 2002

Jiakun Liu

Whether it is Rem Koolhaas/OMA's CCTV Headquarters in Beijing, a rhomboid high-rise for China's largest cable company, or the sleek, black contours of Zaha Hadid's Guangzhou Opera House, a slew of international architects with high-profile projects are shaping China's cultural landscape. Avant-garde forms on a mammoth scale seem to be the status quo for new architecture, yet Chinese architects are reasserting their responsibility in the development of a regional architectural vocabulary. Only since 1995, with the passing of new ordinances, are architects able to emerge from the People's Republic "design institutes" and enter private practice. [14]

Jiakun Liu's design for the Luyeyuan Stone Sculpture Museum validates his nascent artistic and architectural role. Drawing on influences such as Le Corbusier and Carlo Scarpa, Liu introduces a modern language that is wedded to Chinese craftsmanship. Sited along the Fu River in Sichuan Province, the museum displays Buddhist stone sculpture from the Han through Song dynasties: ancient artifacts, some dating back to 206 B.C. The intricate carving on the stone pieces juxtaposes with the coarse concrete surfaces, just as the narrow, vertical windows contrast the solid wall mass. In *Architectural Record*, Liu described this concept as "an architectural story of man-made stone." [15]

Crossing up and over a lotus pond, a long entry ramp penetrates the textured boundary and lands lightly on a catwalk at the museum's second level. Here, poised above the gallery, an interplay of differing scales occurs between sculptures of the Buddha (both small and large) on pedestals and the viewer, now also on a pedestal. (A similar blurring of the relationship between subject and object, sculpture and human, is also seen in Scarpa's renovation of the Castelveccio Museum in Verona.) From here an ambulatory route directs the visitor through the exhibition spaces, wrapping around a roof court and finally descending into the lower galleries.

Although it sits on ground level, there is a subterranean quality to the space. Light enters through slits of glass and skims over the rough concrete. Liu combined local building techniques with his modern lines to create the distinctive walls. In order to ensure straight pours, he outlined the building's footprint in a double layer of shale brick walls, which then acted as formwork for the cement. The bricks left behind a rich pattern, demarcating the complex, intertwined relation between Chinese vernacular construction and contemporary form.

Page 149: Ground-floor gallery
Above: Concrete ramp leading to museum entrance on second level
Opposite, top: South facade
Opposite, bottom: Garden pathway

Above: Gallery interior
Opposite: View along north elevation toward entry ramp

Stone Museum
Nasu, Japan 2000

Kengo Kuma & Associates

Kengo Kuma's Stone Museum is alluringly redundant. Built for the stonecutting company Shirai Sekizai in the Ashino region, an area between Tokyo and Yamgata known for its volcanic stone from Mt. Nasu, it is made out of Ashino stone and displays stone processing and artistry exhibitions. The design defies the heaviness of this repetition; the architect's deft treatment of both site and material brings a studied lightness.

Akin to the children's game "Rock, Paper, Scissors," simple dualities are at play: light/heavy, sharp/rough, new/old. Two prewar farm buildings establish the site, and the rural character of each rough-hewn stone *kura* (rice granary) is mediated by hefty yamizosugi wood bracing, inserted to stabilize the structures. Toward the northeast corner of the museum complex, the smaller existing *kura* serves as an entrance foyer with a café and shop. Beyond the arched doorway, a stone pathway bridges a shallow pool at an angle.

Two elongated L shapes—one a series of reflecting pools and one a composition of stone structures—interlock to form the rectangular compound. The reflecting pools distort the rigor of Kuma's constructs, while the crisscrossing bridges over the water are arranged to give oblique views. The hard right angles are softened by perspective. In an interview in *Architecture* magazine, Kuma discussed his vision to dematerialize structure, turning "stone, a massive material, into a cloud-like substance by transforming it into particles."[14] Kuma's alchemy of making solid material ephemeral is seen in the enclosures that wrap the new gallery spaces like a fabric. The thin walls are made of finely cut Ashino stone; their technological precision contrasts the hand-cut stone of the existing building. Layers of narrow blocks are interwoven with Carrara marble, resulting in a textured wall with horizontal slits. Inside, the translucent apertures glow with patterns of light like a traditional Japanese reed blind.

The new structures—the tea house, the Gallery of Stone and Water, and the smaller Gallery of Stone and Light—are positioned around a plaza. True to the holistic theme of the museum, teacups of *andesaitoh* (a kind of ceramic and stone art) are displayed in the smaller gallery. The pool extends into the Gallery of Stone and Water. Reflections of the bright geometries are mirrored in the dark water, freeing the stone wall from gravity's pull.

The large *kura*, used for special exhibitions or events, fills the far end of the compound and is approached either through the water gallery or via a bridge perpendicular to the entry. While the structure is supported by a wood frame, Kuma retained a gap made by a World War II air raid, letting in light through the rafters. A small gallery on the south side of the compound is partially open to the elements. Protected by a latticework of stone slices on steel framing, it displays different types of stones and quarrying and cutting techniques.

Page 155: Detail of new stone wall abutting stone *kura*
Above: View toward entrance hall
Right: View of museum complex toward exhibition hall

Above and opposite: Gallery of Stone and Water

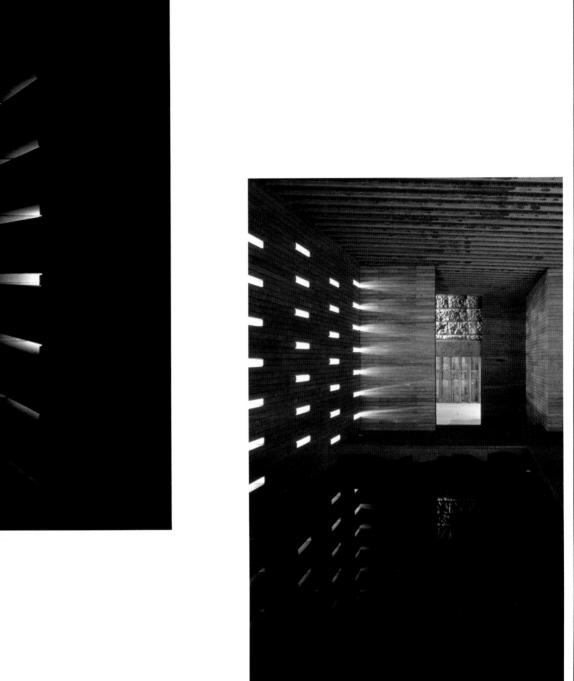

Nasher Sculpture Center
Dallas, Texas 2003

Renzo Piano Building Workshop

The Nasher Sculpture Center is an urban pavilion embedded in the high-rise sprawl of Dallas, Texas. Adjacent to the Dallas Museum of Art, it is part of the downtown Dallas Arts District. Around the 2.4-acre site a postmodern mishmash of shiny office towers juts skyward—strong vertical contrasts to architect Renzo Piano's earthbound design.

The project is a simple diagram: six walls clad in 2-inch-thick Italian travertine extend perpendicularly from Flora Street, forming five glass-vaulted bays. Glazed sidewalk and garden facades produce spatial transparency through the galleries. The architecture of the sculpture museum resists the temptation to express itself as sculpture. Instead, it operates a cultural filter between city bustle and modern art oasis.

It is easy to pinpoint Louis Kahn's Kimbell Art Museum as a reference: the iconic light-filled, vaulted pavilions rightfully set the standard for Texas museum architecture. Yet Piano cites a different architectural touchstone as his inspiration: Roman ruins. The walls sink below grade, creating a second story of galleries for light-sensitive works. An outside amphitheater cuts into the landscape and meets the lower level. The "noble ruins" influence is slightly perverse—antique walls rising out of the Texas asphalt—however, it is in line with the typology of seventeenth- and eighteenth-century folly gardens that functioned as idealized landscapes dotted with sculpture and fabricated "ruins."

The more than three hundred works in the Raymond and Patsy Nasher Collection range from pre-Columbian to modern to contemporary, including pieces by Henri Rodin, Pablo Picasso, Alexander Calder, and Jean Arp. Responding to Raymond Nasher's request, the architect designed glass vaults for the gallery ceilings, which are supported by narrow steel ribs and thin, stainless-steel cables. Floating above the glazing is an intricate sunshade structure. Characteristic of Piano, the sunshades are technologically expressive. Engineered with the help of Ove Arup and Partners, the cast-aluminum oval scoops, set into 4-foot-by-6-inch arrays, funnel north light into the spaces.

Outside exhibition space is six times bigger than the total inside gallery space (which shares square footage with a library, offices, and a café). Designed by landscape architect Peter Walker, the garden extends the museum into a pastoral setting and neatly picks up the modern archaeological theme. Low travertine walls alternate with reflecting pools and rows of live oaks and cedar elms. The garden culminates in a James Turrell "skyspace," a site-specific artwork that frames a piece of Texas firmament, making a spiritual connection between earth and sky.

Page 161
Top: Terrace and outdoor theater at night
Bottom: Entry facade

Above: Sculpture garden facade
Opposite: Reflecting pool with Henry Moore's *Working Model for Three Piece No 3: Vertebrae* (1968) in foreground

Above: View toward museum with Mark di Suvero's
Eviva Amore (2001) installed in sculpture garden
Right: Gallery with sculptures by Alberto Giacometti

Modern Art Museum of Fort Worth
Fort Worth, Texas 2002

Tadao Ando

For any museum, comparison with Louis Kahn's masterpiece the Kimbell Art Museum is a mark of distinction. But a commission to build a museum on a lot adjacent to that iconic structure of limestone, concrete, and light—and thus have one's work compared to it daily—is a dubious honor to be reckoned with. Designed by Tadao Ando, the Modern Art Museum of Fort Worth stands one block west of the Kimbell's vaulting galleries, and without mimicking Kahn's building, Ando succeeds in evoking its classical, high modernist tone.

The 153,000-square-foot museum sits on an 11-acre landscaped site. Although it is the largest museum displaying modern art outside of New York City, its scale is revealed in layers. "My intent was to create and oasis, a place where visitor can engage with art both inside and outside the museum," Ando has written of the structure.[17] Trees shelter the museum from the street, and out of the grove rises the long, horizontal stretch of the building. The restrained facade mediates Fort Worth's suburban sprawl and the artwork it contains. At the center of the elevation the regular grid of aluminum panels gives way to glass panes supported by aluminum mullions and organized along the same datum. Two elongated concrete columns flank the main entrance like sentinels, but the gallery pavilions can be glimpsed through the glass.

Floor-to-ceiling windows in the main lobby reveal Ando's second "layer" of exterior elevations. Three glass-sheathed boxes seemingly float on the 1.5-acre pond. Their flat roofs with outstretched eaves hover, touching down lightly on Y-shaped concrete columns that rise like abstract trees out of the reflecting pool, extending several feet in front of the glass facade. The tripling of the boxes recalls the steady cadence of concrete semi-circles at the Kimbell. However, where Kahn's rhythms created a structural system that allowed for long spans of columnless gallery space, Ando's architecture continues a longstanding exploration of the dualities of built form versus nature and interior versus exterior space.

The gallery pavilions make up the short side of the L-shaped museum plan. Inside each is a second box, a more enclosed art space. In Ando's original scheme, these were autonomous concrete volumes, but, confronted with Texas building techniques, Ando reconfigured them as gypsum board with concrete columns. The galleries are large and airy, some even double height, and all are lit with natural light. Varied gallery configurations make visitors continually aware of the natural surroundings. The glass skin wrapping the pavilions forms porchlike, ambulatory space around the galleries and filters the light reflecting off the water.

Inside the galleries, works by Donald Judd, Andy Warhol, and Anselm Kiefer epitomize the range of modern art from Abstract Expressionism to Pop. A similar aesthetic range emerges unintentionally in Ando's modernist landscape. A concrete wall encloses the museum site, ending the long view across the pond and embracing the abstracted natural setting; yet peeking over the boundary are several billboards and a winking Texaco sign.

Page 167: View of galleries across reflecting pond
Above: Exterior view
Right: View of museum café and lobby from gallery

Pages 170–71: North gallery behind glass curtain wall
Above: Entrance lobby
Opposite: Grand stair to second-floor exhibition spaces

Nevada Museum of Art
Reno, Nevada 2003

William Bruder

Located at the meeting of the eastern edge of the Sierra Nevada Mountains and the expanse of the High Desert, the "Biggest Little City in the World" has an uneasy relationship with its landscape. Gold rush mineshafts riddle the foothills, while Reno's casino strip boasts storefront wedding chapels and nickel slots. Against this eclectic backdrop stands the Nevada Museum of Art (NMA), Donald W. Reynolds Center for the Visual Arts, E. L. Wiegand Gallery, designed by Arizona architect Will Bruder. A swooping gesture in black zinc, the building sits like an artifact in a grid of office buildings and porch-fronted houses.

The formal design of the museum was inspired in part by the black rock formations located a couple of hours outside of Reno in the High Desert. The NMA's curving, striated wall resembles the geologic layering of a dark convex mesa. Rising out of a ground-level sculpture garden, the folded zinc wall, supported by nine steel columns, dramatically tilts from 5 to 12 degrees depending on the viewer's location. "The building is a sculpture, part of the museum's collection," says Bruder of the four-story metal facade. "I knew it had to be black, because we were in a town of ephemeral, pale, and turquoise buildings."[18]

Less severe than the exterior, the interior is shocking in its lightness. A white atrium allows for the play of bright spots and shadows. Galleries spiral around a metal stairway suspended by a single beam in the atrium ceiling. Transitions from floor to floor and between galleries are surprisingly casual. Interior windows and openings give the space a fluid transparency. "The building is like a camera that the photographers use on the landscapes," explains Bruder. "The surrounding buildings respond to the museum, each talking about its own time in history." Each floor offers a different view of the city. The second-floor windows frame details of nearby houses and panoramic views of the neighborhood. At the third level, the rake of the windows mimics the rake of the mountain range on the horizon.

"The Altered Landscape," a large piece of the NMA's permanent collection, provided rich conceptual material for the architect to draw upon. The collection, begun in 1998, features contemporary landscape photography whose imagery describes the topography of the West: nuclear test blast sites and mine shafts, military bases, and sprawling suburbs. The parapet walls of the 8,000-square-foot Nightingale Rooftop Gallery rise and fall to block or reveal that landscape. The largest opening offers an idealized perspective of Reno, while another outdoor room frames nothing but the sky. Bruder's sensitivity to context allows for a building that is an object, a gestural sculpture, but one that is also connected to the Wild West mythology of its haphazard landscape.

Page 175: Facade viewed from sculpture plaza with Nancy Dwyer's *Inhale/Exhale* (2002)
Above: Permanent gallery designed for Robert Beckmann's *Body of a House* (1993)
Right: Atrium

Above: Entrance to museum offices with Frederic Tchorbadjian's *Stainless Spin* (2003)
Opposite: Nightingale Rooftop Gallery with Ilan Averbuch's *Shadow of the Sun* (2003)

Bellevue Arts Museum
Bellevue, Washington 2000

Steven Holl Architects

A red cube faceted with storefront windows, the Bellevue Arts Museum (BAM) stands across the street opposite its former home in the Bellevue Mall. Prior to its mall-rat phase, the museum, which developed out of a street art fair, was housed in a school and then a funeral home. The quotidian nature of these spaces carries over to the new structure, along with an idiosyncratic program. There is no permanent collection; rather, the museum's mission stresses education and features community art classrooms, a ceramics studio, artist-in-residence studio space, and a library, in addition to temporary exhibition galleries.

A Seattle suburb that has grown with the tech industry, the city of Bellevue experienced a boom coinciding with the dot-com bubble. The bubble burst as the museum opened in 2000, and two and a half years later BAM closed its doors. However, at the time of writing plans are in place for the museum to reopen in spring 2005.

BAM is positioned to bring density to the loose fabric of downtown Bellevue, and Steven Holl has described the project as a "prototype for urbanizing a sprawling suburban zone."[19] Mixing a bit of social reform in with his design for the edge-city museum, he envisions its architecture as an agent of transformation, reinvigorating civic space through art activities and culture rather than the staples of suburban life: shopping and driving. By placing parking for the museum underground, Holl allows the building to confidently meet the sidewalk with an active corner entry, awnings, and café seating.

The museum's disparate functions are brought together in the Forum, a white, lozenge-shaped void formed by stairs rising around its perimeter. While similar to the Kiasma's sweeping atrium, it is a more tightly coiled space lacking the Finnish museum's sublime payoff. Holl refers to this space as a "social condenser"—a space where programs overlap. A short staircase with deep treads leads to a landing that doubles as a stage or lectern for public events. From there a straight stair, bending slightly at its apex, brings the visitor to the second floor, which contains a mix of administrative offices, studios, and support facilities.

A glass stair, whose graceful arc disappears around a bend, reaches the third story, spilling visitors out into the Court of Light, an open terrace that functions as an exhibition space for sculpture and as a venue for projections of experimental video work at night. On this floor a tripartite composition of three "lofts" houses studios and galleries. Mystically, Holl equates the quality of light in each loft with the nature of time: the even north light in the first loft is identified with "Linear Ongoing Time"; "Cyclic Time" represents the second loft, whose curved plan and skylight follows the angle of the sun at 48 degrees latitude; the third loft embodies "Gnostic Time," or fragmented time. Additional terraces adjacent to the galleries fill the space between the oblique gallery walls and the orthogonal floors and street grid below.

Page 181: Rooftop Court of Light
Above: West facade
Opposite: View of atrium from entry

Below: Staircase connecting second floor to rooftop sculpture court
Opposite: North light gallery

Moderna Museet
Stockholm, Sweden 1998

Rafael Moneo

Unpresumptuous and refined, the Moderna Museet delicately responds to light and context. So modest is it, in fact, that when the building was temporarily closed for renovations due to damp, mold, and poor air quality, you could imagine the architecture blushing from embarrassment. Designed by Spanish architect Rafael Moneo, the newly reopened museum assimilates into the topography of the island of Skeppsholmen. Originally a base for the Swedish navy, the island is lined with nineteenth-century barracks and maritime buildings, many of which have been converted to cultural intuitions. Moneo takes advantage of these historic structures: his building unifies them into a larger complex.

Moneo chose a rocky outcropping for Moderna Museet, carving it into the steep grade to reduce the appearance of overall mass. Viewed from the harbor, the museum's east elevation takes on the texture of the island vernacular. Square windows puncture the terra-cotta-colored facade, echoing the naval buildings' fenestration. The gallery pavilions rise out of the gridded base, with their pyramidal roofs lining the ridge. Clustered below the octagonal dome and cupola of the church completed by Fredrik Blom in 1853, and which is now used by the museum as a lecture hall, the roofs glow at night like lanterns.

A simple, low portico marks the museum's public entrance on the west, uphill side. The plan follows the adjacent flank of the narrow former rope factory that is now the Museum of Oriental Antiquities. Linked by a wide corridor, the galleries sprawl across the ground floor, with the administrative offices, cinema, and library tucked into the subterranean spaces cut into the rock below.

Squares and rectangles cluster in three groups to form the permanent collection galleries. Within each pavilion six or seven rooms interlock into a maze of top-lit spaces. The intricate circulation between each space enriches the plain white walls and oak floor trimmed in limestone. The arrangements are true to the easy complexity characteristic of Moneo's work, which can also be seen in his design for the Beck Building of the Museum of Fine Arts in Houston (2000).

The lanterns that jauntily cap each room along the roofscape are subdued on the interior. Filtered natural light enters the galleries through louvers. The temporary exhibition hall modifies the lantern motif. A matrix of thirty smaller lanterns tops the large, flexible volume.

While the new galleries present modern art, a renovated navy drill hall serves as the Swedish Museum of Architecture. Here an architectural archive and library is also designed by Moneo. Its streamlined white form, a slightly different motif from the gallery pavilions, is scaled to complement the historic buildings on the site. The variety of old and new structures engage elegantly with the surroundings to complete rather than fragment the collage along the harbor.

Page 187: Detail of north facade
Above: Panoramic view of Skeppsholmen Island
Right: Courtyard looking toward former navy drill hall

Above: Corridor connecting galleries
Opposite: Temporary exhibition gallery

Museu Serralves
Oporto, Portugal 1999

Alvaro Siza

Alvaro Siza is a master at manipulating bright, Portuguese sunlight. His forms, modernist derivations, modulate seemingly endless gradations of shadow and light. At the Museu Serralves, the Cubist outcropping of shifting, white planes fold along a gentle slope, catching the light. The museum sits on the grounds of the Quinta de Serralves, a sprawling 1930s estate with vast lawns and formal gardens dominated by a grand, pink Art Deco villa that previously housed the Serralves Foundation. Established in 1989, the foundation rapidly expanded its collection of post-1960s art and outgrew the original building. To avoid competing with the villa's architecture, Siza's project is set away from the house in a former vegetable patch and takes its orientation from the direction of the furrows.

Access to the museum is through an elegant gate set into the original estate stone wall. Here begins Siza's languid approach to circulation—ample time and space are given to the *promenade architecturale*. A long, covered walkway leads the visitor past a pavilion, along the walled edge of the compound, and squeezes past the corner of the auditorium. That compression gently opens to a patio between the main exhibition building and the theater. The exterior room is an eddy in the circulation route, a momentary pause at which to shift one's attention from the expansive vistas overlooking the estate garden in anticipation of viewing artwork.

A generous square skylight formalizes the central atrium, which, in turn, is the hub for the H-shaped parti. Arranged along a single axis, the space maintains a classical tone, but Siza is not content with standard symmetries. The composition of spaces is balanced and modern, yet pleasingly off-kilter. Each of the wings develops its own character. On the west side the circulation blends with the exhibition space, creating a diagonal flow between the adjacent volumes, while to the east a corridor isolates two large galleries, ending in an ensemble of smaller rooms. Linking the two wings is a double-height hall. Rather than introducing a single beaux-arts stair on axis, Siza uses a switchback ramp to change levels in the room and balance the inequity of the two wings.

The galleries are illuminated by a variety of methods. Some are illuminated by standard skylights, while others receive daylight filtered by what look like oversized, inverted coffee tables that act like soffits, washing the walls in reflected light from a concealed skylight. These tablelike structures, which seem to hover in space, are an invention carried over from Siza's design for the Galician Center for Contemporary Art (1993) in Santiago de Compostela, Spain.

The bulk of the 140,000-foot compound is nearly invisible. Offices and storage drop into the site on two floors below the exhibit spaces. Siza continually reconnects the building back to the garden with balconies and windows that frame and control views like a camera, linking the building to the landscape.

Page 193: Covered entrance into museum compound
Pages 194–95: Main entry ramp at north facade
Above: Courtyard between museum and auditorium
Opposite: View of south facade from garden

Above: Gallery with soffit-like skylights
Opposite: Gallery

Tang Teaching Museum and Art Gallery at Skidmore College
Saratoga Springs, New York 2000

Antoine Predock

Described as an "interdisciplinary arts center," the Tang Teaching Museum and Art Gallery provokes the question, What are the formal attributes of interdisciplinary design? The museum, as a representation of the liberal arts institution Skidmore College, required a building both flexible and rich in complexity. Antoine Predock answered with a scheme of intersections: three wings and two circulation paths converge around a central space. For the architect these intersections speak to a larger philosophical expression. "The Teaching Museum and Art Gallery is designed to articulate the fundamentally inseparable connection of art to human culture and consciousness," states Predock on his Web site.

Sited on the edge of the Skidmore College campus, the Tang serves both the college and the city as the first art museum in Saratoga Springs. Predock's design is expressive of both academic and civic communities. Operating as a built interpretation of a crossroads metaphor, two dramatic exterior walkways—a 140-foot steel staircase and a 120-foot concrete staircase—meet on an upper-level deck. Low slung, but slowly rising to a symbolic "ivory tower," the building is modestly scaled. A quiet cement block faces Saratoga Springs, while the collegiate facade is clad in textured steel panels.

Predock is hyperaware of the environmental context as well as the cultural context of the museum. Much of his work in the Southwest draws on natural features: rocky desert plains, mesas, and the vast horizon. The Tang is his first building in the Northeast, and although Predock draws inspiration from geological forces, evoking limestone caves at Skidmore College, the scenery is subtle and modestly scaled. But Predock makes the most of the site by situating the museum in a circle of white pine trees. The ramplike stairways tie the structure to the ground and reach out along preexisting pathways toward other campus buildings.

Inside the museum a large atrium links the building's various circulation paths and provides a conceptual link for the museum program's various disciplines. The ceiling, echoing the rise of the exterior, slopes from 14 to 34 feet. The central space is a nexus for the museum's functions—the curatorial offices, classrooms, archive, temporary and permanent collection galleries, and a 2,200-square-foot "interdisciplinary space" flexible enough for performances, exhibitions, or fundraising banquets.

Page 201: Exterior steel staircase leading to upper-level deck
Above: Facade facing campus
Opposite: View of bridge across atrium

Above: Ground-floor gallery with Nick Cave's *Sound Suits* (2003)
Opposite: Atrium

Notes

Introduction

1 Andrew Friedman, "Build It and They Will Pay: A Primer on Guggenomics," *The Baffler* 15 (February 2003): 51–56.
2 Jayne Merkel, "The Museum as Artifact," *The Wilson Quarterly* 26, no. 1 (Winter 2002): 66–79.
3 Ibid.
4 James Traub, "The Stuff of City Life," *New York Times Magazine* (October 3, 2004): 23–29.
5 Ibid.
6 Friedman, "Build It and They Will Pay."
7 Rem Koolhaas, "Junkspace," in *Content*, by OMA/AMO and Rem Koolhaas (Cologne: Taschen, 2004).
8 Ibid.
9 Ibid.
10 Merkel, "The Museum as Artifact."
11 Larry Flynn, "7 New Trends in Museum Design," *Building Design and Construction Magazine* (December 2002): 24–30.
12 Ibid.

Project Descriptions

1 Steven Holl, *Parallax* (New York: Princeton Architectural Press, 2000).
2 Steven Holl and Jussi Tianen, *Kiasma, Museum of Contemporary Art* (Helsinki: Finnish Building Society, 2001).
3 Doris Erbacher and Peter Paul Kubitz, interview in *Jewish Museum Berlin*, by Daniel Libeskind (New York: G+B Arts International, 1999).
4 Clifford A. Pearson, "MOMA QNS," *Architectural Record* (August 2002): 109.
5 Yoshio Taniguchi, interview with Terence Riley, Museum of Modern Art press materials.
6 Robin Pogrebin, "At Modern, Architect is content (Mostly)," *New York Times*, November 16, 2004, sec. E, p. 3.
7 Peter Zumthor, *Kunsthaus Bregenz* (New York: Distributed Art Publishers, 1999).
8 Adolf Max Vogt, "Étienne-Louis Boullée Visits the Tate Modern," in *Herzog & de Meuron: Natural History*, edited by Philip Ursprung (Baden, Switzerland: Lars Müller Publishers, 2002).
9 Ruth Keffer, "Dia:Beacon, *loud paper* Interviews Architect Linda Taalman," *loud paper* (Spring 2004).
10 "Lost and Finding: An Interview with Kazuyo Sejima and Ryue Nishizawa," *Hunch: The Berlage Institute Report* 199, no. 1 (Autumn 1999): 144–51.
11 Eugenia Bell, ed., *Shigeru Ban* (New York: Princeton Architectural Press, 2000).
12 Hans Hollein, "Digging and Piling Up," on his Web site, www.hollein.com.
13 Eric Strain, interview by author.
14 Nancy Levinson, "Future Present," *Architectural Record* (March 2004): 74.
15 Clifford A. Pearson, "Luyeyuan Stone Sculpture Museum," *Architectural Record* (March 2004): 88.
16 Michael Webb, "Particle Theory," *Architecture* (March 2003): 66.
17 *Tadao Ando: Light and Water* (New York: Monacelli Press).
18 Will Bruder, interview by author.
19 Jean Pastier, "Urbanism Cubed," *Metropolis* (June 2001): 96.

Photography Credits

Resources

Contemporary Art Museum
3750 Washington Boulevard
St. Louis, Missouri 63108
(314) 535-4660
www.contemporarystl.org

Pulitzer Foundation for the Arts
3716 Washington Boulevard
St. Louis, Missouri 63108
(314) 754-1850
www.pulitzerarts.org

Kiasma, Museum of
Contemporary Art
Mannerheiminaukio 2,
FIN-00100
Helsinki, Finland
(358) 9-1733-6501
www.kiasma.fi

Contemporary Arts Center
The Lois and Richard Rosenthal
Center for Contemporary Art
44 East Sixth Street
Cincinnati, Ohio 45202
(513) 345-8400
www.contemporaryartscenter.org

Jewish Museum
Lindenstraße 9-14
10969 Berlin, Germany
(49) 30-25993-300
www.jmberlin.de

American Folk Art Museum
45 West Fifty-third Street
New York, New York 10019
(212) 265-1040
www.folkartmuseum.org

Museum of Modern Art, Queens
(MoMA QNS)
Long Island City
Queens, New York
www.moma.org

Museum of Modern Art
11 West Fifty-third Street
New York, New York 10019
(212) 708-9400
www.moma.org

Kunsthaus Graz
Lendkai 1
A-8020 Graz, Austria
(43) 316-8017-9200
www.kunsthausgraz.at

Museum of Modern Art—Ludwig
Foundation (MUMOK)
Museumsplatz 1
A-1070 Vienna, Austria
(43) 1-525-00
www.mumok.at

Kunsthaus Bregenz
Karl Tizian Platz
A-6900 Bregenz, Austria
(43) 5574-48594-0
www.kunsthaus-bregenz.at

Tate Modern
Bankside
London SE1 9TG, England
(44) 20-7887-8000
www.tate.org.uk/modern

Dia:Beacon
3 Beekman Street
Beacon, New York 12508
(845) 440-0100
www.diabeacon.org

O-Museum
Iidashi Ogasawara Shiryoukan
3942-1 Izuki
Iida, Nagano, Japan

Kalkriese Archaeological Museum
Park
Vennerstraße 69
49565 Bramsche-Kalkriese,
Germany
(49) 5468-92040
www.kalkriese-varusschlacht.de

Paper Art Museum
Shizuoka, Japan
(81) 055-988-2401
http://tokushu-paper.jp

Art Pavilion "De Verbeelding"
De Verbeelding 25
3892 HZ Zeewolde, Netherlands
(31) 36-5227037
www.verbeelding.nl

Makino Museum of Plants and
People
Shikoku Island, Japan
(81) 088-882-2601
www.makino.or.jp

Echigo-Matsunoyama Museum of
Natural Science
Matsunoyama, Japan
www.matsunoyama.com/kyororo

De Young Museum
75 Tea Garden Drive
Golden Gate Park
San Francisco, California 94118
(415) 750-3600
www.deyoungmuseum.org

Vulcania: Parc Europeen du
Volcanisme
Route de Mazayes
F-63230 Saint-Ours les Roches,
France
(33) 4-73-19-70-10
www.vulcania.com

Mesquite Heritage Museum and
Art Center
15 East Mesquite Boulevard
Mesquite, Nevada 89027

Luyeyuan Stone Sculpture
Museum
Yun Qiao, Xinmin
611732 Sichuan Province, China
(86) 28-87926835

Stone Museum
2717-5 Nakamachi, Ashino,
Nasu-machi
Tochigi 329-3443, Japan
(81) 287-74-0228
www.stone-plaza.com

Nasher Sculpture Center
2001 Flora Street
Dallas, Texas 75201
(214) 242-5100
www.nashersculpturecenter.org

Modern Art Museum of Fort
Worth
3200 Darnell Street
Forth Worth, Texas 76107
(817) 738-9215
www.themodern.org

Nevada Museum of Art
160 West Liberty Street
Reno, Nevada 89501
(775) 329-3333
www.nevadaart.org

Bellevue Arts Museum
510 Bellevue Way NE
Bellevue, Washington 98004
(425) 519-0770
www.bellevueart.org

Moderna Museet
Skeppsholmen
Stockholm, Sweden
(46) 8-5195-5200
www.modernamuseet.se

Museu Serralves
Rua D. João de Castro, 210
4150-417 Porto, Portugal
(351) 22-615-6500
www.serralves.pt

Tang Teaching Museum and Art
Gallery at Skidmore College
815 North Broadway
Saratoga Springs, New York
12866
(518) 580-8080
tang.skidmore.edu